IMAGO DEI

Seeing Yourself Through
Your Father's Eyes

DONNA CULPEPPER

Trilogy Christian Publishers
A Wholly Owned Subsidiary of Trinity Broadcasting Network
2442 Michelle Drive
Tustin, CA 92780
Copyright © 2024 by Donna Culpepper
Scripture quotations marked ESV are taken from the ESV® Bible (The Holy Bible, English Standard Version®), copyright © 2001 by Crossway Bibles, a publishing ministry of Good News Publishers. Used by permission. All rights reserved. Scripture quotations marked MSG are taken from THE MESSAGE, copyright © 1993, 2002, 2018 by Eugene H. Peterson. Used by permission of NavPress. All rights reserved. Represented by Tyndale House Publishers, Inc. Scripture quotations marked NIV are taken from the Holy Bible, New International Version®, NIV®. Copyright © 1973, 1978, 1984, 2011 by Biblica, Inc. TM Used by permission of Zondervan. All rights reserved worldwide. www.zondervan.com. The "NIV" and "New International Version" are trademarks registered in the United States Patent and Trademark Office by Biblica, Inc.TM Scripture quotations marked NLT are taken from the Holy Bible, New Living Translation, copyright © 1996, 2004, 2015 by Tyndale House Foundation. Used by permission of Tyndale House Publishers, Inc., Carol Stream, Illinois 60188. All rights reserved. Scripture quotations marked NKJV are taken from the New King James Version®. Copyright © 1982 by Thomas Nelson. Used by permission. All rights reserved. Scripture quotations marked KJV are taken from the King James Version of the Bible. Public domain.
All rights reserved, including the right to reproduce this book or portions thereof in any form whatsoever.
For information, address Trilogy Christian Publishing
Rights Department, 2442 Michelle Drive, Tustin, Ca 92780.
Trilogy Christian Publishing/TBN and colophon are trademarks of Trinity Broadcasting Network.
For information about special discounts for bulk purchases, please contact Trilogy Christian Publishing.
Trilogy Disclaimer: The views and content expressed in this book are those of the author and may not necessarily reflect the views and doctrine of Trilogy Christian Publishing or the Trinity Broadcasting Network.
10 9 8 7 6 5 4 3 2 1
Library of Congress Cataloging-in-Publication Data is available.
ISBN 979-8-89041-671-1
ISBN 979-8-89041-672-8 (ebook)

Dedication

This book is dedicated to my husband, Steve. Without all that you have done, I would not have been able to spend time on our back porch listening to God's voice and writing His story. This book is also dedicated to my parents, who taught my brother and me to love the Word of God and the importance of Scripture memory from a very young age. To my boys: being your mom has been the greatest gift of my life. I didn't always get it right, but God's grace stepped in, and you have become wonderful young men of integrity and honor and the most excellent daddies. I also dedicate this story to my tribe. You knew my story and encouraged me for years to write a book. You prayed for me through the process and shared loving words of wisdom… We did it!

Most of all, thank You, Jesus, for never giving up on me… *Soli Deo gloria!* (Glory to God alone.)

Table of Contents

Introduction: Imago Dei 1
Chapter 1: Third Grade 5
Chapter 2: Grasshoppers 10
Chapter 3: Gorilla Glue 14
Chapter 4: The Mountain Dew Test 19
Chapter 5: Call Me Gomer? 25
Chapter 6: Invisible 30
Chapter 7: Hey, Big Fella! 34
Chapter 8: Tick Tock 39
Chapter 9: Ironman 45
Chapter 10: 4-H 49
Chapter 11: Label Maker 53
Chapter 12: Backpacking 58
Chapter 13: The Kid's Table 62
Chapter 14: Walker, Texas Ranger 67
Chapter 15: DQd 73
Chapter 16: Two Fish Sandwiches 78
Chapter 17: The Brady Bunch Goes to the Grand Canyon 84
Chapter 18: A Trip to Fantasy Island 91
Chapter 19: Judge Judy 97
Chapter 20: Masterpiece 103
Chapter 21: Two Little Words 110
Chapter 22: Lost Luggage 116

Chapter 23: Jesus and Naps 120
Chapter 24: Chanel Perfume 126
Chapter 25: YMCA 131
Chapter 26: One Big Lie 137
Chapter 27: Dogs Do Fly 142
Chapter 28: The Dance 149
Chapter 29: Grace Received 156
Chapter 30: Grace Begins at the Cross 159
Chapter 31: I Love Free Stuff! 165
Chapter 32: The Greatest Invitation *Ever*! 171
Conclusion: The Call 177
Endnotes 182

Introduction

Imago Dei

> He has made everything beautiful in its time. He has also set eternity in the human heart; yet no one can fathom what God has done from the beginning to end.
>
> Ecclesiastes 3:11 (NIV)

As I sit down to write this, I see my image reflected on my laptop screen. It's an early Saturday morning, no make-up, dirty hair...undone. I am horrified by my reflection...until I whisper the words, "*Imago Dei*." This phrase has become key in my transformation from an ugly duckling to a beautiful daughter of the King. Did my physical appearance or figure change? No, but my vision did...because of *imago Dei*: the image of God. This is my third attempt at writing a book over the past few years (different topics). But this is the one area in my life that I have struggled with the most and keep coming back to. So, it must be the topic that I am the most "expert" at. Everybody has a story. Everybody has "that thing" that they are insecure about. The world tells us that we are not enough, but our Creator Redeemer tells us that we are created in His image (*imago Dei*). That, ladies, means we are *more* than enough.

In this book, I will present you with a lie or label that the Enemy tries to put on us, and then I will take you back to Scripture and debunk that lie with the truth of who God says we are. This book is a fast read. It reads like a collection of short essays. His grace (my redemption) calls for me to be real, honest, transparent, and a tad bit vulnerable. My life has been messy, but His grace has been greater. When His Word goes out, it never returns void, and this book is chock-full of His Word. We will use it to see ourselves through His eyes. Have a seat in your most comfy chair, get your Bible out, pour yourself a cup of coffee or tea, and let's discover together why we are beautiful, worthy daughters of the King.

Question: *Imago Dei*...where did I come up with those words?

Answer: I didn't. Lisa Harper did! Well, she really didn't, but she is the one who introduced me to those words. I am a voracious reader, and she is one of my favorite Christian authors. Her books really resonate with me. A little over a year ago, Lisa started a podcast called *Back Porch Theology*[1], and that is where I was introduced to this new term. It kept resounding in my head, and I began to use it as a weapon against the Enemy.

Imago Dei is Latin for "image of God." We all know that Genesis 1 is the creation story in the Bible. Every step of the way, when God created (from nothing) something new, He characterized the created as "good." That is until He got to the creation of mankind:

> So God created mankind in His own image, in the image of God He created them; male and female He created them.
>
> Genesis 1:27 (NIV)

This is where we are introduced to the words *imago Dei*.

It wasn't until after the creation of man and woman

(Adam and Eve) that God called His creation *very* good:

> God saw *all* that He had made, and it was *very* good. And there was evening, and there was morning—the sixth day.
>
> Genesis 1:31 (NIV, author's italics)

So, wait…if God created me in His own image and He thought His creation was *very* good, then am I calling His baby "ugly" when I entertain negative self-talk about myself and my appearance? Hmmm… I never really thought about it that way—lots to ponder there.

This is the beginning of my journey into digging deep and finding out what God really says about me, maybe yours as well. My dear friend, Angela, just texted me a good word about this process, "He doesn't need you to write a book. He wants you to draw so close to Him that you can hear His breath. Then, it's His words." Thank you for the reminder, Angela.

> Show me your ways, Lord, teach me your paths. Guide me in your truth and teach me, for you are God my Savior, and my hope is in you all day long.
>
> Psalm 25:4–5 (NIV)

God calls us to be storytellers (His story) and not story keepers. Perhaps your story is the same as mine. Perhaps you've allowed Satan and the world to define you and tell you who you are. Satan is a deceiver. He tries to define us in order to hold us back from being all that we were created to be. But we have a secret weapon. We are *imago Dei*… created in God's very own image. That gives us power and purpose. Our story (of restoration and redemption) is all for His glory. Let's work together to change the narrative of our lives. We are *imago Dei*, and our collective stories will bring Him glory!

> We're listening, Lord.
>
>> And now, dear brothers and sisters, one final thing. Fix your thoughts on what is true, and honorable, and right, and pure, and lovely, and admirable. Think about things that are excellent and worthy of praise.
>>
>> Philippians 4:8 (NLT)

Chapter 1

Third Grade

But godliness with contentment is great gain.

1 Timothy 6:6 (NIV)

Third grade. That is when I was put on my first diet. I can remember what the doctor's office looked like. I can still hear the doctor's antiseptic voice, "We've got to get a hold of this now, or she will struggle her entire life." Words hurt. Words last forever. Words resound in your mind over and over. That's when it began. That's when I *knew* I was different. That's when I began to want to look like everybody else. That's when the sin of comparison crept into a little girl's heart. (And we didn't even have the internet, Facebook, Instagram, or TikTok back then!)

Theodore Roosevelt said, "Comparison is a thief of joy." God never meant for us to compare ourselves to others. God took great joy in making each one of us unique. You've heard it over and over, probably all your life. "God made you on purpose for a purpose." There's no one like you, and no one can fulfill God's calling on your life but you!

I've heard it all my life…in one ear and out the other. The voice inside my head was louder than my mom's, my Sunday school teacher's, or even God's.

IMAGO DEI

What does God really say about me? Well, to start with, He says that I am beautifully and wonderfully made. (Insert eye roll emoji...I've heard it as long as I can remember, and it has *not* been helpful...up until today.) I have been familiar with parts of Psalm 139, but I don't think I really *knew* the meaning of Psalm 139 until I read it in another translation and sat with it for a minute.

> Oh yes, you shaped me first inside, then out;
> you formed me in my mother's womb.
> I thank you, High God—You're breathtaking!
> Body and soul, I am marvelously made!
> I worship in adoration—what a creation!
> You know me inside and out,
> you know every bone in my body;
> You know exactly how I was made, bit by bit,
> how I was sculpted from nothing into something.
> Like an open book, you watched me grow from
> conception to birth;
> all the stages of my life were spread out before
> you,
> The days of my life all prepared
> before I'd even lived one day.
>
> Psalm 139:14–16 (MSG)

What an amazing translation! This passage is David's praise party for how he was created. I bet you're saying, "Of course, he is praising God for how he was created." Earlier in the Bible, we are told that David was "glowing with health and had a fine appearance and handsome features" (1 Samuel 16:12b, NIV). God does not spend a lot of time in the Bible defining people's physical appearance, so David must have been a looker to get that kind of recognition. But...David had other issues that might have caused him to feel insecure and unworthy. In 1 Samuel 17, Goliath saw that David was just a boy, meaning he was probably small in stature. That certainly is not a feature that men are envious of. We know from other areas in the Bible that David had some character flaws. For instance, his leadership failure caused him to sin with Bathsheba, which set off a series of heartbreaking events. The bottom line is that we all have "stuff" about ourselves that we are insecure about, even David. Yet…he praised God for how he was made.

Let's *break* down Psalm 139 a bit:

> Oh yes, you shaped me first inside, then out; you formed me in my mother's womb.

David recognized who his Creator was. He recognized that before he even existed, God was his architect and artist. God was planning David's existence. He was designing what David would look like. He was designing his body, soul, and mind. He was designing that David would be a "man after His own heart." He *knew* David and shaped him in his mother's womb like a sculptor shapes a work of art. Oh, my goodness, is it not mind-blowing that God has done that very act of design and sculpting billions and billions of times over? Every person that ever existed or ever will exist…over and over and over. Unique and special. The world census, as of January 1, 2022, was estimated to be over 7.8 billion people! That's just a drop in God's bucket at how many times He created or will create a human being. Each one is unique and treasured…simply mind-blowing.

> I thank You, High God—You're breathtaking!
> Body and soul, I am marvelously made!
> I worship in adoration—what a creation!

Here, David tells God that He (God) is breathtaking.

God is perfect, without flaw. We can't even imagine what He looks like. We know that His appearance was so holy and brilliant that Moses had to hide his face.

> "Do not come any closer," God said. "Take off your sandals, for the place where you are standing is holy ground." At this, Moses hid his face, because he was afraid to look at God.
>
> Exodus 3:5, 6b (NIV)

David appreciated the beauty of God's creation and worshiped the Creator. He knew he was made in the image of God, *imago Dei*. So, he *must* be marvelously made as well.

> You know me inside and out,
> you know every bone in my body;
> you know exactly how I was made, bit by bit,
> how I was sculpted from nothing into something.

Again, God had a plan. He had a design. He knew David when David was just a thought. He designed David perfectly according to His plan.

I moved to the country about four years ago. I decided I wanted to be a "farmer," so I planted a vegetable garden in three eight-foot raised beds. I planted tomatoes, jalapenos, cucumbers, zucchini, and green beans. I also planted a ton of marigolds because I learned that flowers are essential in attracting pollinators, a necessary ingredient for growing vegetables. Every morning and every evening, I love to go out and "inspect the crops" to see what God has done. It gives me great joy to watch the circle of life in my tiny garden. How much more joy it must give our Heavenly Father to watch the circle of life in His creation:

> Like an open book, you watched me grow from
> conception to birth;
> all the stages of my life were spread out before
> you,
> The days of my life all prepared before I'd even
> lived one day.

Jeremiah 29:11 (NIV) reinforces that last sentence:

> "For I know the plans I have for you," declares
> the Lord, "plans to prosper you and not to harm
> you, plans to give you hope and a future."

Don't you love the consistency throughout the Bible? He designed us just the way we are *on purpose, for a purpose*, and He has a good plan for each and every one of us…all 7.8 billion of us! *Imago Dei*, made in His image.

Chapter 2

Grasshoppers

> We don't see things clearly. We're squinting in a fog, peering through a mist. But it won't be long before the weather clears and the sun shines bright! We'll see it all then, see it all as clearly as God sees us, knowing him directly just as he knows us!
>
> 1 Corinthians 13:12 (MSG)

How I see myself affects every area of my life: my spiritual life, my relationships with other people, my work life, etc. If I still see myself as that chubby little third-grade girl, constantly comparing myself to others, I will never fulfill God's plan for my life. I have found out that how I have viewed myself all these years is very different than how others have viewed me. My view of myself has proven to be self-limiting. I did not take risks or put myself out there for fear of rejection or defeat. I forgot, or perhaps I did not know, *imago Dei*. I was made in the image of God.

Grasshoppers…what? Yes! I was reminded of this story in Sunday school this morning. There is a story in the Bible where a group of men saw themselves as grasshoppers, which ultimately led to their demise. Let me take you there:

In Numbers 13–14, we join Moses as he sends twelve

spies out to explore Canaan. He asked them to check out the people and the land. "Are the people strong or weak? Is the land good or bad? Are there any obstacles in the way of taking the land?" He told them to come back and report to him. I find it interesting that he sent twelve spies out to explore the land. Why twelve? Why not just two or three? He surely would get twelve different opinions. I guess he wanted representation from every tribe, so he sent twelve.

> They gave Moses this account: "We went into the land to which you sent us, and it does flow with milk and honey! Here is its fruit. But the people who live there are powerful and the cities are fortified and very large."
>
> Numbers 13:27–28 (NIV)

It sounds like their perception of the inhabitants of Canaan was that they were giant-ish. But Caleb (known as a fearless leader) had a different impression of the same land and people. We pick it up in verse 30:

> Then Caleb silenced the people before Moses and said, "We should go up and take possession of the land, for we can certainly do it."
>
> Numbers 13:30 (NIV)

Well, that is a very different interpretation of the situation!

> But the men who had gone up with him said, "We can't attack those people; they are stronger than we are." And they spread among the Israelites a bad report about the land they had explored.
>
> Numbers 13:31–32 (NIV)

> We seemed like grasshoppers *in our own eyes*
> and we looked the *same to them*.
>
> Numbers 13:33 (NIV, author's italics)

Full stop. Their perception of themselves was that they were grasshoppers in comparison to the Canaanites. Who told them that? God certainly did not tell them that. Had God not been telling them (and showing them) throughout their journey that He was a *big* God and He would deliver them? Had He not promised them this land? It would not matter how big or small they were physically because God was fighting for them! He had proved it repeatedly. But they were stubborn people.

Not only was their self-confidence in the basement, but they also assumed that their opponents saw them as grasshoppers as well. I can't tell you how many times I have made comments about my self-perception to my husband or friends, and they don't see what I see. I project my poor self-image onto others and assume they see me that way as well. That is what the ten spies did. They assumed the Canaanites saw them as conquerable, weak grasshoppers. It did eventually lead to their demise, but not in the way that you think:

> So the men Moses had sent to explore the land, who returned and made the whole community grumble against him by spreading a bad report about it—these men who were responsible for spreading the bad report about the land were struck down and died of a plague before the Lord.
>
> Numbers 14:36–37 (NIV)

Yikes! Their inaccurate self-image led to an inaccurate perception of what their enemies thought of them, which ultimately led to them being struck down by a plague. Pretty harsh, right? God cares about what we think about ourselves! I find it interesting that in these two verses, the words "spreading a bad report" were repeated. When something is repeated in the Bible, we need to pay attention. Their poor self-perception stole their confidence and caused them to drag others down with them! Think about it! There were 600,000 or so men on the Exodus journey. When you add in women and children, there was probably a total of around two to three million people! Their negative report spread like wildfire throughout the whole community of sojourners.

What a big "aha!" moment for me. Has my own poor self-perception and insecurity poisoned people around me? Ouch! God cares about how we perceive ourselves. Comparison is a sin in which we often find ourselves falling short, and it gives us an inaccurate view of others and of God. God created us in His image *(imago Dei)*, and it is a sin to call His baby (His creation) ugly.

Chapter 3

Gorilla Glue

> Do not let any unwholesome talk come out of
> your mouths, but only what is helpful in building
> others up according to their needs that it may
> benefit those who listen.
>
> Ephesians 4:29 (NIV)

Gorilla Glue! It's my secret weapon. I don't glue bowling balls, as seen in the TV commercial, but I do find myself reaching for it often. It can glue anything. It is super sticky, quick to set in, and its strength will hold fast. Kind of like...words! Remember the childhood phrase, "Sticks and stones may break my bones, but words will never hurt me?" I am here to tell you (as a bullying survivor) the opposite is true. When you break a bone, the calcification during the healing process actually makes the point of breaking stronger. That is not so with words. Words cut deep. Words are locked away in our memory, and Satan the Accuser likes to dig them up at the most opportune times.

We'll call her Anna...my nemesis in grade school and junior high. Looking back now, I realize that she must have been an unhappy person because "hurt people hurt people," right? She was awful to me. She would make fun of me and call me names (fat, cow, etc.) in front of everybody in the cafeteria. This went on for years. I would come home crying. Finally, my mom went to her mom to talk about the bullying, and my mom ended up getting bullied, too. That shed light on the whole situation. We know and act upon what we live. She did not live in a home of peace and encouragement like I did. She lived in an unhappy home, and it played itself out at school.

> For the mouth speaks what the heart is full of. A good man brings good things out of the good stored up in him, and an evil man brings evil things out of the evil stored up in him.
>
> Matthew 12:34b–35 (NIV)

Ugly words are a heart issue. When I say ugly things about others, it speaks to the condition of my own heart. As I write this, I am convicted. Scenes flash through my mind's eye like a movie, showing me times when I have said ugly or untrue things about others. Gossip…it's also a heart issue. It doesn't just hurt the one that I am spreading a rumor about; it hurts me. It is usually the result of my own insecurities, trying to make me feel better about myself. Satan the Accuser *loves* gossip. He *loves* to keep dissension and disunity stirred up. Our words are one of his weapons of choice.

I was Anna's target, and her words carried on into my adulthood. As a result, I became my own harshest critic. Poor self-image became Satan the Accuser's favorite weapon to hold me back. For most of my life (and I still struggle with it today), I have "given the enemy a seat at my table," a table that has been set for just me and Jesus. I have let Satan the Accuser define me and tell me who I am. And it all started with a hurt little girl's hateful words.

I remember, as a child, singing a chorus in Sunday school that said, "Oh, be careful little tongue what you say." It was a warning to us as small children that words have power. Words cut. Words last. Let's see what *the Word* says about the wisdom found in holding our tongues.

> The wise store up knowledge but the mouth of a fool invites ruin.
>
> Proverbs 10:14 (NIV)

> One whose heart is corrupt does not prosper; one whose tongue is perverse falls into trouble.
>
> Proverbs 17:20 (NIV)

> When words are many, sin is not absent, but he who holds his tongue is wise. The tongue of the righteous is choice silver, but the heart of the wicked is of little value. The lips of the righteous nourish many but fools die for lack of judgment.
>
> Proverbs 10:19–21 (NIV)

I'm sure you have heard the old adage that women use way more words than men. If you went on my girls' beach trip with me and six of my BFFs, you would notice that that is, in fact, true! My husband does not understand how we can go to the beach and sit in our beach chairs, staring at the waves and talking for seven straight hours every day for a week. It makes absolutely no sense to him. (That is why he and the other husbands are not invited.) Informal research (via Siri…LOL!) suggests that women spend about 20,000 in word currency a day versus men at 5000–7000 words. I have no idea if that is true. I know some women who spend way more than 20,000 words and some who spend very little. The bottom line is (according to Proverbs) that the more words we speak, the more likely we are to sin (say things that are untrue or hateful). Wisdom is found in choosing our words wisely and spending them sparingly.

> Those who consider themselves religious and yet do not keep a tight rein on their tongues deceive themselves, and their religion is worthless.
>
> James 1:26 (NIV)

I find it interesting that God connects wisdom with holding our tongues in many of these verses. Just because we think it does not mean we have to say it. A wise woman pauses and thinks about what is about to spill out of her mouth. Remember? Out of the contents of your heart comes the words of your mouth (my paraphrase).

I am reminded of my mom. She is a precious, sweet, servant's heart kind of lady. She has always been friendly, chatty, and so encouraging to everyone she meets. I laugh when I think about the story of her and my dad at the 1996 Summer Olympics in Atlanta. Mom's forte has always been her servant's heart, always eager to help. They were at an outdoor sporting event in the crowded stands, watching the athletes do their thing. There was a lady sitting next to them with quite a big purse loaded to the max. The lady made the comment that she needed to get up and go to the restroom. My mother, being the servant-hearted individual that she is, volunteered to hold the *complete stranger's* purse for her while she went to the bathroom. At that, the lady jumped up, grabbed her purse, and fled. That's my mom, always the helpful one. If Mom thinks it, she speaks it. I always get amused with her, but in all reality, my filter is becoming a little lax these days as well. "Mirror, mirror on the wall...I am my mother, after all!"

"Oh, be careful, little tongue, what you say..."

I know it is hard to ignore and deposit what others say about us where it belongs (in the trash can), but it really doesn't matter. The only opinion I should be concerned about is what my Father in heaven thinks of me. We are *imago Dei*...made in His image...only His opinion of us counts.

Chapter 4

The Mountain Dew Test

> Direct your children onto the right path, and
> when they are older, they will not leave it.
>
> Proverbs 22:6 (NLT)

We were your typical nuclear family of the '60s and '70s...dad, mom, one brother, one sister. My parents introduced us to Jesus at an early age. We were in the church nursery from day one. One of my dad's favorite stories to tell was of my brother misbehaving in big church. My mom was a pincher. She would pinch us in situations where we were supposed to be quiet and still. My dad would turn his college class ring around and rap us on the head. (He was a rapper before there was such a thing!) One particular Sunday, my pre-school-aged brother had ants in his pants. Mom had pinched, and Dad had rapped. My brother let out a yelp during the sermon, "Ouch! That hurt!" Sentencing and punishment were swift and decisive in my family. (There were no negotiations.) Mom swooped him up and took him out into the lobby of the church, and...let's just say the whole church heard it, and the pastor probably said, "Amen!"

I recently found out that my precious brother had become a Gideon. When I was growing up, God's Word took center stage in our home, so it is quite fitting for him to join the organization that hands out Bibles all over the world. Who is this Gideon fella of the Bible? Since my brother joined the Gideons, I decided that I needed to know more:

We find the story of Gideon in Judges 6 and 7. Chapter 6 starts out with a familiar statement, "The Israelites did evil in the eyes of the Lord..." (Judges 6:1, NIV). For seven years, God gave the Israelites over to the hands of the bully Midianites. Everything the Israelites planted, the Midianites would plow up. They would kill the Israelites' livestock. Basically, they were trying to starve the Israelites through the destruction of their food supply.

Gideon was hiding from the Midianites under a tree, using a winepress to thresh his wheat, making it fit to eat. An angel of the Lord showed up and said to Gideon,

> The Lord is with you, *mighty warrior*.
>
> Judges 6:12b (NIV, author's italics)

Gideon's response was classic in verse 13 (author's paraphrasing):

"Pardon me, my lord," Gideon replied, "but if the Lord is with us, why has all this happened to us?"

Two things stand out to me in this verse: First, it appears that Gideon did not see himself as a *mighty warrior*. He was sitting under a tree, having a pity party, and giving the Enemy a seat at his table. The scripture doesn't say it, but the Enemy was probably whispering in his ear, "Mighty warrior? Ha!" Because that is what the Enemy likes to do. He likes to contradict who God says we are. The second thing I noticed is that Gideon really was a whiner. He had forgotten all the times in the past when God had delivered the children of Israel and could only see the here and now, which was not great.

> The Lord turned to him and said, "Go in the *strength you have* and save Israel out of Midian's hand. Am I not sending you?"
>
> "Pardon me, my lord," Gideon replied, "but how can I save Israel? My clan is the weakest in Manasseh, and *I am the least in my family.*"
>
> Judges 6:14–15 (NIV, author's italics)

Poor Gideon. He was in need of hearing aids. *Twice*, he said to God, "Pardon me, am I hearing You right?" I bet God wanted to reply, "What do you not understand about the word 'go'?" Again, Satan the Accuser was telling Gideon, "You are just a small-town boy, and you are the weakest guy in your family!" Satan *loves* to define us! But we are *imago Dei*, created in the image of God! We can do *all things* through our God, who strengthens us!

Gideon, listen to God! He is telling you to go in the strength that you *already* have. (Me plus Jesus is a majority!) He will equip you because *He* is sending you! In verse 16, God *again* tells Gideon that He will be with him.

But Gideon still suffers from hearing loss in verse 17,

> Gideon replied, "If now I have found favor in your eyes, give me a sign that it is really you talking to me."
>
> Judges 6:17 (NIV)

In the next few verses, Gideon prepares an offering of unleavened bread and meat. God touched the offering and made a fire flame up from the rock, and the offering was burned up. Gideon was impressed and built an altar and called it "The Lord Is Peace." Was that show of strength enough for Gideon to press on in the Lord's power? I think not!

> Gideon said to God, "If you will save Israel by my hand as you have promised—look, I will place a wool fleece on the threshing floor. If there is dew only on the fleece and all the ground is dry, then I will know that you will save Israel by my hand, as you said." And that is what happened. Gideon rose early the next day, he squeezed the fleece and wrung out the dew—a bowlful of water.
>
> Then Gideon said to God, "Do not be angry with me. Let me make just one more request. Allow me one more test with the fleece, but this time make the fleece dry and let the ground be covered with dew." That night God did so. Only the fleece was dry and all the ground was covered with dew.
>
> Judges 6:36–40 (NIV)

The Mountain Dew test...not once, but twice. Satan the Accuser's voice was louder in Gideon's head than the voice of God. Gideon believed who the Enemy said he was more than He believed how big his God was! Watch what a great big God can do when we finally obey, believe who He says we are, and believe just how *big* He is:

> The Lord said to Gideon, "You have too many men. I cannot deliver Midian into their hands, or Israel would boast against me, 'My own strength has saved me.' Now announce to the army, 'Anyone who trembles with fear may turn back and leave Mount Gilead.' So twenty thousand

left, while ten thousand remained.

But the Lord said to Gideon, "There are still too many men. Take them down to the water and I will thin them out for you there. If I say, "This one shall not go with you" he shall not go." So Gideon took the men down to the water. There the Lord told him, "Separate those who lap the water with their tongues as a dog laps from those who kneel down to drink." Three hundred of them drank from cupped hands, lapping like dogs. All the rest got down on their knees to drink.

The Lord said to Gideon, "With the three hundred men that lapped I will save you and give the Midianites into your hands. Let all the others go home!"

Judges 7:2–7 (NIV)

And as they say...the rest is history. God used 300 Israelites to defeat the vast army of the Midianites. He showed up *big* on Gideon's and the Israelites' behalf. The children of Israel had no choice but to give God the credit for the great big victory that they had just experienced.

Question: Why do you think that God chose the soldiers who did *not* kneel down and drink from the stream?

Answer: The soldiers who drank from cupped hands were still on guard. Their eyes were still on the enemy. They were ready and aware.

What did I learn from this story? Well, three things, really. The first is the most important: my God is a great *big* God and can do anything with anybody. The second thing I learned is that I need to turn my hearing aids up and drown out the voice of the Enemy. I need to believe that I am who God says that I am! *Imago Dei!* And finally, when I come to a spring of fresh, clean water, I should lap the water from my cupped hands instead of kneeling down to drink. Interesting!

Chapter 5

Call Me Gomer?

> Yet I hold this against you: You have forsaken the love you had at first. Consider how far you have fallen! Repent and do the things you did at first.
>
> Revelation 2:4–5a (NIV)

When I hear the name Gomer, I think of Gomer Pyle, the goofy Marine on the '60s sitcom. (I am aging myself right here. You millennials might need to Google that one.) In the Bible, Gomer is a woman...a rather promiscuous woman at that. Hosea is one of the good guys. He is a prophet and takes God at His Word. Hosea trusts God's heart. So, when God tells Hosea to go marry a woman of ill repute, Hosea is immediately obedient. Personally, I would have probably bargained with God a little bit, "God, I have done all the right things. I have followed You. I have proclaimed You to a deaf and sinful world. My reward is to marry this loosey-goosey woman? Are You sure that's Your best for me?" But Hosea did just the opposite:

> When the Lord began to speak through Hosea, the Lord said to him, "Go marry a promiscuous woman and have children with her, for like an adulterous wife this land is guilty of unfaithful-

> ness to the Lord." So he married Gomer daughter of Diblaim, and she conceived and bore him a son.
>
> Hosea 1:2–3 (NIV)

Gomer bore Hosea three children. Check out their names:

> Call him Jezreel, because I will soon punish the house of Jehu for the massacre at Jezreel, and I will put an end to the kingdom of Israel.
>
> Hosea 1:4 (NIV)

The second child was a girl, and God told Hosea to name her Lo-Ruhamah, which means "not loved." Along with Lo-Ruhamah's name came a promise:

> Yet I will show love to Judah; and I will save them—not by bow, sword or battle, or by horses and horsemen, but I, the Lord their God will save them.
>
> Hosea 1:7 (NIV)

A second son was born after Lo-Ruhamah, and Hosea named him Lo-Ammi, which means "not my people." Again, with this name came a promise:

> Yet the Israelites will be like the sand on the seashore, which cannot be measured or counted. In the place where it was said to them, "You are not my people," they will be called "children of the living God."
>
> Hosea 1:10 (NIV)

God uses the story of Gomer to illustrate that Israel had become promiscuous and had left its first love (Him). He used the story of Gomer to illustrate redemption. Of course, as you would expect, Gomer left Hosea and the kids and "looked for love in all the wrong places."

This is where I think I might be Gomer. No, I didn't carouse around and live a life of promiscuity. But I did, for ten years, walk away from Jesus, my first and truest love. Oh, I still went to church, prayed, and occasionally blew the dust off my Bible, but the relationship was just not there. I went through a divorce (two to be exact) and made a series of not-great choices based on how I viewed myself (rejected, unloved, and unworthy). I hate, with everything in me, to admit that I am twice divorced. But without admitting it, you will not see the bigness of my redemption story. Gomer probably also had a pretty rotten view of herself, felt unworthy, and made choices based on that. Gomer and I both forgot our true identities: that we were chosen and dearly loved by God.

After Gomer's partying days were over, she went on the auction block to be sold as a slave. I don't know if one of her lovers put her on the block to be sold or if she put herself on the block to be sold, thinking nobody (especially Hosea) would want her. But God told Hosea to bring her back.

> The Lord said to me, "Go, show your love to your wife again, though she is loved by another man and is an adulteress. Love her as the Lord loves the Israelites, though they turn to other gods and love the sacred raisin cakes."
>
> So I bought her for fifteen shekels of silver and about a homer and a lethek of barley.

IMAGO DEI

Hosea 3:1–2 (NIV)

Hosea bought Gomer back at a pretty high price. In today's terms, a shekel of silver is equal to about five dollars. A homer was about six bushels, and a lethek was about three and a half bushels. So, Hosea bought her back for about seventy-five dollars and nine and one-fourth bushels of barley. It doesn't sound like much, but it probably amounted to quite a hefty sum in those days. What was even more costly to Hosea was the hurt, shame, and embarrassment that he and his children had to endure when Mama left to experience the world.

Redemption is costly to the Redeemer. My redemption was costly to my Redeemer, and so was yours. God's story of redemption is quite consistent throughout the Old and New Testaments. In the Old Testament, the Israelites strayed from God and followed false gods. God made a way for them to come back to Him over and over again. In the New Testament, God's ultimate act of redemption entered the world in the person of Jesus. Jesus paved the path of reconciliation for us at a very high price...His own life.

> God so loved the world that He gave His one and only Son, that whoever believes in Him shall not perish but have eternal life. For God did not send his Son into the world to condemn the world, but to save the world through him.
>
> John 3:16–17 (NIV)

Like Hosea, Jesus was obedient to fulfill God's redemption story, no matter the price. Paul tells us twice in the New Testament that we were bought at a high price.

> Do you not know that your bodies are a temple

> of the Holy Spirit, who is in you, whom you
> have received from God? You are not your own;
> you were bought at a price. Therefore honor God
> with your bodies.
>
> 1 Corinthians 6:19–20 (NIV)

First Corinthians 7:23 also tells believers that we were bought at a price and tells us not to become slaves to the world. (Don't let the world define us!)

First Peter 1:18–19 (NIV) tells us more about that price:

> For you know that it was not with perishable
> things such as silver or gold that you were
> redeemed from the empty way of life handed
> down to you from your ancestors, but with the
> precious blood of Christ, a lamb without blemish
> or defect.

There is an old hymn that says, "Jesus paid it all, / all to Him I owe. / Sin had left a crimson stain, / He washed it white as snow."[2] Gomer's redemption was costly. But she now had new names: redeemed, dearly loved, worthy. My redemption was costly. I, too, have new names: redeemed, dearly loved, worthy. Your redemption was costly as well, and you have those same new names. We were created in His image, *imago Dei*, and we were created for relationship with our Creator Redeemer.

Gomer, no more.

Chapter 6

Invisible

> The eyes of the Lord are on the righteous, and
> his ears are attentive to their cry.
>
> Psalm 34:15 (NIV)

Have you ever felt invisible? For a good part of my life, I felt like I was invisible. I felt "not seen." There really was no reason for feeling like that; I guess it just stemmed from my own view of myself. It was just another label that Satan, the Deceiver, gave me. Unfortunately, I bought into that lie.

I have been a pharmaceutical rep for going on thirty years. Oh, the stories I could tell about my adventures (and misadventures) as a sales representative! One story comes to mind as I think about feeling invisible. I began calling on Dr. Henry (fictitious name) in the late '90s. He was a family practice physician in a small town in the country, about sixty miles away. Dr. Henry liked to play games with reps. You would stand by his nurse's station and wait for him to stop so you could give him a brief pearl of information about your medication. He would walk by you about five times before he would stop, listen, and give you a quick signature for samples. I never got more than a grunt of recognition from him. One particular day, I had had enough and boldly asked him, "Can you see me? Am I invisible?

You have been walking by me for years without the slightest bit of recognition. I was just wondering if I am invisible to you?" With that, he gave a great big belly laugh and said, "I wondered when you would finally say something to stop me in my tracks!"

It's a funny story, but we can often feel invisible. Sometimes, we can feel lonely in the middle of a crowded room. That's when Satan likes to whisper in our ears, "Nobody likes you. Nobody wants to talk to you. You're not special. You're invisible." (Remember walking into the cafeteria in school, panicked about where to sit or who would sit with you?)

Hagar must have felt like she was invisible. The story of Hagar is told in Genesis Chapter 16. Remember the backstory? Abram and Sarai (soon to be renamed Abraham and Sarah) were getting old and did not yet have any children. When I say old, I mean super old, like they should have been great-grandparents by now. But God promised Abram that He would build a great nation from his and Sarai's children:

> He took him outside and said, "Look up at the sky and count the stars—if indeed you can count them." Then he said to him, "So shall your offspring be."
>
> Genesis 15:5 (NIV)

Abram believed God...but Sarai became impatient. She decided to give Abram her servant, Hagar, to conceive children with. Abram made a stupid mistake and acquiesced to Sarai's offer. Hagar, indeed, became pregnant...but Abram was about to pay for it (another blame game in the Bible.) Abram couldn't win.

> He slept with Hagar, and she conceived.
>
> When she knew she was pregnant, she began to despise her mistress. Then Sarai said to Abram, "You [*blame game*] are responsible for the wrong I am suffering. I put my slave in your arms, and now that she knows she is pregnant, she despises me. May the Lord judge between you and me."
>
> "Your slave is in your hands," Abram said. "Do with her whatever you think best." Then Sarai mistreated Hagar, so she fled from her.
>
> Genesis 16:4–6 (NIV)

Well, that's a sticky situation...all because Sarai became impatient waiting for God to fulfill His promise. Pregnant Hagar runs away and is found by an angel sitting near a spring in the desert. The angel calls her by name (a sign of knowing and a sign of respect) and asks what she is doing. She explains her situation and why she has run away. The angel tells her to return to Sarai and submit to her. He promises Hagar that she will have many descendants. Don't you know that Hagar felt invisible? She felt like nobody could see her in her calamity. She felt (and was) alone. After the angel reveals all of God's promises to her, she makes this statement,

> She gave this name to the Lord who spoke to her, "You are the God who sees me," for she said, "I have now seen the One who sees me."
> That is why the well was called Beer Lahai Roi; it is still there, between Kadesh and Bered.
>
> Genesis 16:13–14 (NIV)

She was seen by God. She was no longer invisible. As an added bonus...she saw the One (capital "O") who sees her...God. Is it not mind-blowing that out of all the billions of people ever created, God sees me? He is El Roi, the God who sees me. He knows my name:

> Do not be afraid, for I have ransomed you. I have called you by name; you are mine.
>
> Isaiah 43:1b (NLT)

He cares about every tear that I shed:

> You keep track of all my sorrows. You have collected all my tears in your bottle. You have recorded each one in your book.
>
> Psalm 56:8 (NLT)

I am not invisible (and neither are you). I was not invisible to good old Dr. Henry, and I am certainly not invisible to *El Roi, the God who sees me*. After all, He created me in His own image (*imago Dei*), and He's not likely to forget me.

Chapter 7

Hey, Big Fella!

> But the Lord said to Samuel, "Do not consider his appearance. or his height, for I have rejected him. The Lord does not look at the things people look at. People look at the outward appearance, but the Lord looks at the heart."
>
> 1 Samuel 16:7 (NIV)

I love the story of David, the scrawny shepherd boy who would become king. I find myself always rooting for the underdog. (Maybe because I have always considered myself somewhat of an underdog.) I really get into March Madness. I love it when the underdog, the 16-seed, wins their way to the Sweet 16, Elite 8, or perhaps even Final 4. I always cheer them on (except, of course, if they are playing against my beloved Arkansas Razorbacks.)

I'm pretty much a sports gal. I enjoy watching football, basketball, baseball, and golf. Both of my boys played sports in college, so I have quite a background in being a spectator. My youngest was quite a standout as a defensive end (football) in high school. He won all-state in the 7A West in Arkansas his senior year. He went on to play D2 college football. He had a handicap, though; he was considered small in stature, which kept him from playing D1 ball. He had the moves and the speed, and he was strong as an ox. But...his misfortune was in his DNA. My dad (who also played college football) was five foot three; my mom is four foot ten. I also am no giant, measuring in at a mere five foot two. He had no chance in the height department. It is so unfortunate that college coaches only look at outward appearance, in particular, height and weight. What they missed in all those recruiting visits was his heart. He had a heart, a work ethic, and a love for the game that was unrivaled.

Our favorite movie of all time is the true story of Rudy Ruettiger. We loved the movie so much that we named our puppy Rudy! Rudy was a short little guy with a great big heart and a passionate love for the Notre Dame football team. He was from a steelworker family that could not afford to put him through college. He worked his tail off to make it first to junior college (to get his grades up) and ultimately to Notre Dame. Rudy walked onto the Notre Dame football team. He made it through the cuts, not because of his size or skill, but because of the size of his heart. The movie chronicles his football career there...on the scout team. His goal was to help his fellow teammates be better by challenging them on the field as a member of the scout team. But he still had one remaining goal...to step foot onto the field during a game before he graduated.

Rudy became discouraged toward the end of his senior year. The season was about to wrap up, and it did not look like he was going to step onto that field and officially go down in the record book as having played for Notre Dame. In his frustration, he quit. When he found out that he had quit, his older friend (who was the stadium groundskeeper) had a few choice words for Rudy:

> You're 5-foot nothin', 100 and nothin', and you

> have nearly a speck of athletic ability. And you hung in there with the best college football team in the land for two years. And you're gonna walk outta here with a degree from the University of Notre Dame. In this life, you don't have to prove nothin' to nobody but yourself.[3]

If you know how the story ends, you'll know Rudy does step onto the field. He makes some spectacular tackles with seconds left in the game. I believe that no other Notre Dame football player since has been carried off the field on the shoulders of his teammates. Rudy went down in Notre Dame football history and became a much sought-after motivational speaker.

Rudy made history. Rudy did not listen to the lies of the Enemy, and he did not care what others thought of him. We have a similar Rudy story in our family. The coach who recruited my son to his college team left a year or so after he began to play there. The new positional coach only looked at his stature, not his ability or his heart. After sitting out most of his senior year due to shoulder surgery, they put him in during the last game. He made his signature moves around the opponents and made some stellar tackles. It. Was. Cold. Chills. He was so impressive that the coach who never gave him a shot asked him to come back for his fifth year of eligibility. He said no.

When my son was playing high school football, before every game, I would say, "Not by might, not by power," and he would return with, "But by the Spirit of the Lord." His story and Rudy's story both remind me of the story of David and Goliath. Looking at David, he was an unlikely warrior. He was a shepherd who played the harp. He had zero battle experience. Like Rudy, he was probably "5-foot nothin' and a 100 and nothin'," but he had a great big heart for the God he loved.

Goliath was a nine-and-a-half-foot-tall giant of a man. His armor weighed 125 pounds. The iron point of his spear weighed 15 pounds. For forty days, Goliath taunted the Israelites and their God. That did not sit well with David. He told Saul that he would fight the giant and win. Saul's response was that he was just a boy. David's response was:

> Your servant has killed both the lion and the bear; this uncircumcised Philistine will be like one of them, because he has defied the armies of the living God. *The Lord who rescued me from the paw of the bear will rescue me from the hand of the Philistine.*"
>
> Saul said to David, "Go and the Lord be with you."
>
> 1 Samuel 17:36–37 (NIV, author's italics)

You see, David didn't see Goliath as a giant; he saw the God of Israel, his God, as a giant! Perception is everything! David knew his God would be faithful because He had always been faithful in the past.

You know how the story goes. Saul tried to outfit him with his own personal armor, but David could not walk in it. He tried to give him his weapons, but David had better weapons in mind:

> Then he took his staff in his hand, chose five stones from the stream, put them in the pouch of his shepherd's bag and, with his sling in his hand, approached the Philistine.
>
> Meanwhile, the Philistine, with his shield bearer in front of him, kept coming closer to David. He looked David over and saw that he was little

> more than a boy, glowing with health and handsome, and he despised him. He said to David, "Am I a dog, that you come at me with sticks?" And the Philistine cursed David by his gods.
>
> 1 Samuel 17:40–43 (NIV)

(Just a side note here because I have never noticed it before: it says that Goliath had his shield-bearer *in front* of him. That seems like a pretty wimpy move to me, don't you think?)

David replies that Goliath comes to fight with sword and spear, but he, David, comes against Goliath and his armies in the name of the Lord Almighty. David *ran* toward the challenge (Goliath), took out a stone, and slung it toward Goliath. It hit Goliath in the middle of the forehead, and he fell to the ground.

No. Sword. Needed!

(No sword was needed to kill Goliath, but David did use Goliath's sword to cut off his head.)

How big is your God? Do you let the Enemy tell you that you are too small, that you can't do something, or that you are unworthy? David *ran* toward the challenge because he *knew* that his God was bigger than anything he would come up against. David ran toward the challenge because he *remembered* what God had done for him in the past. David ran toward the challenge because he was *imago Dei*, made in the image of God, and God would equip him with all that he needed...if only he believed. You, too, are *imago Dei*...just believe.

Chapter 8

Tick Tock

> Now if we are children, then we are heirs—heirs of God and co-heirs with Christ if indeed we share in his sufferings in order that we may also share in his glory.
>
> Romans 8:17 (NIV)

Read the chapter title again... "Tick Tock," not "Tik-Tok." One was a rhyme from my playground in the '70s, and the other is an attention-getting social media app from today. The first one is hurtful, and the pursuit of the second can be hurtful, as well.

> Tick Tock, the game is locked, and
> nobody else can play.
> And If you do, we'll take your shoe
> and that will be the end of you!

Surely, that playground rhyme was a precursor to the hit movie *Mean Girls*. Why was that movie such a big hit? It's probably because it resonated with so many of us girls. Perhaps our mean girl experiences were not that epic, but we still had our times of not belonging, most likely beginning on the playground.

There are several versions of that childhood rhyme, all with an exclusive and ugly meaning. I remember hearing it on the playground. I remember saying it on the playground. I would like to say that this kind of exclusivity ends when we leave childhood. Unfortunately, that is not the case. It still goes on, and it still hurts. Sometimes, it happens at work. Sometimes, it happens in families. Sometimes, it happens in a group of friends. Sometimes...it even happens at church.

I can remember a few scenarios in my life when I felt like I didn't belong. Perhaps you can relate to a couple. The first one was, of course, on the playground when I was excluded from a playground game. (Although, I was always chosen first for Red Rover because I was somewhat chunky for a girl and could break those hands!) We moved from New Mexico when I was in eighth grade. I remember that panicky feeling of who I would sit with in the lunchroom at my new school. At college, I joined a sorority so I would have a sense of belonging. Even at church as an adult, I wanted to sing in the choir so badly, but I didn't have anybody to sit with. (I quickly overcame that fear as my love for singing overcame my fear of not fitting in.)

The Enemy would like us to believe the lie that "I don't belong" or "I am not a part." What happens when we believe that lie? We isolate ourselves from others. I just looked in the dictionary for synonyms for the word "isolate." Words like aloneness, seclusion, segregation, and separateness were all listed.

Interestingly enough, none of those words are listed in the Bible as a fruit of the Spirit. Satan loves to isolate us. If he can isolate us, he has unencumbered access to our brains. If he can make us feel like we don't belong or we don't fit in, he has us.

Remember when Jesus was tempted in the wilderness? He was alone, just Jesus and Satan. The Deceiver tried to get into Jesus's head and tempt Him four times. Four times, he was unsuccessful. Why? Because Jesus fought Satan's lies with the truth of the living God. (A theme expressed all throughout this book.)

We do belong. The Word tells us that we belong to Him:

> And the Lord has declared this day that you are his people, his treasured possession.
>
> Deuteronomy 26:18 (NIV)

The Word tells us that we are chosen:

> You did not choose me, but I chose you and appointed you so that you might go and bear fruit—fruit that will last—and so that whatever you ask in my name the Father will give you.
>
> John 15:16 (NIV)

The Word tells us that we are adopted:

> But when the set time had fully come, God sent his Son, born of a woman born under the law, to redeem those under the law, that we might receive adoption to sonship…
>
> So you are no longer a slave, but God's child; and since you are his child, God has made you also an heir.
>
> Galatians 4:4–5, 7 (NIV)

Let's dig into that adoption part for a moment. Adoption

is special. When parents adopt a child, they *choose* that child to be a part of their family. They *choose* that child to do life with. They *choose* that child to love unconditionally. That is what it means to be adopted: *chosen*. In biblical times, a Jewish parent could disown or disinherit a natural born child; however, it was illegal to do that with an adopted child. That is how special adoption was then and how special it still is today. The Bible tells us that by being adopted into God's family, we are joint heirs with Christ. Now that's a really big deal!

A great example of adoption in the Bible is in the books of First and Second Samuel. After David killed the giant, he was brought into King Saul's house to live. Jonathan (Saul's son) and David became the best of friends. The Bible says they were like brothers.

> After David had finished talking with Saul, Jonathan became one in spirit with David and he loved him as himself. From that day Saul kept David with him and did not let him return home to his family. And Jonathan made a covenant with David because he loved him as himself.
>
> 1 Samuel 18:1–3 (NIV)

Fast forward a few years. Saul tries to kill David. Jonathan warns David and helps him hide. Saul eventually dies, and David becomes king. Jonathan was killed in battle when his son, Mephibosheth, was a kindergartner. (We'll call him Meph for short.) Meph's nurse becomes scared for his life and runs away and hides him. As they are running, Meph trips and falls and becomes lame. Fast forward several years:

> The king asked, "Is there anyone still alive from

> the house of Saul to whom I can show God's kindness?" Ziba answered the king, "There is still a son of Jonathan; he is lame in both feet."
>
> 2 Samuel 9:3 (NIV)

David summoned Meph to come before him. Don't you know that given the history between David and his grandfather, Meph might have been just a tad bit nervous?

> When Mephibosheth son of Jonathan, the son of Saul, came to David, he bowed down to pay him honor.
>
> David said, "Mephibosheth!"
>
> "At your service," he replied.
>
> "Don't be afraid," David said to him, "for I will surely show you kindness for the sake of your father Jonathan. I will restore to you all the land that belonged to your grandfather Saul, and you will always eat at my table."
>
> 2 Samuel 9:6–7 (NIV)

In Jewish tradition, whoever you break bread with becomes your family. By David offering Mephibosheth a seat at his table, he was actually extending an offer to become a permanent part of his family. Not only did he adopt him into his family, but he also restored to him all his family's wealth, treasure, and status. He *belonged*.

That is what God does for us when He adopts us into His family. The scripture says that we become heirs of God and co-heirs of Christ (Romans 8:17). If we are born-again believers, we become His children through adoption. We have full access to the greatest inheritance ever! *We belong!*

So, Satan can try to isolate us all he wants. He can tell us that we don't belong. But we know better. We are *imago Dei*, and that means we are chosen; we are His treasured possession, and we are adopted into His family.

Chapter 9

Ironman

In his heart a man plans his course, but the Lord determines his steps.

Proverbs 16:9 (NIV)

I had to think long and hard about what character I would consider to be my favorite superhero. I'm not really a Marvel Universe fan, so coming up with a favorite was a bit of a stretch. I think it must be Ironman because I really did enjoy those movies. I do love me some Tony Stark (Robert Downey, Jr.) and Pepper Potts (Gwyneth Paltrow). Ironman had a sense of humor and didn't take himself too seriously, and I like that. So…Ironman it is.

I have my own superpower. It is one that I have probably possessed since birth. My superpower is overthinking. I overthink, overanalyze, and over-ruminate (is that a word?) *everything*! In my morning quiet time, I often confess the stronghold of overthinking. I overanalyze what others think of me. I overanalyze my to-do list at work. I overanalyze my travel and plot my most efficient route. I rehearse conversations. I project worst-case scenarios. (etc., etc., etc.) As I said, I overthink *everything*, and I am very, very good at it! Last Saturday, I hosted a family birthday party for my son. I planned and cooked for two days. Everything. Was.

Perfect. Do you know what my mom's comment was about my hosting abilities? "You are so very efficient!" Yikes! Did she have fun with all my efficiency? (I found out later that she, in fact, did.)

Recently, during my quiet time, as I was yet again confessing the sin of overthinking, Jesus showed me that overthinking is, indeed, an idol. You see, *anything* that we obsess over is an idol because it takes our focus from Him and places it elsewhere. Ouch! In my striving to be *perfect*, I take my eyes off the prize (Jesus). Flashback to Sunday school memory verse:

> As the Scriptures say, "No one is righteous—not even one."
>
> Romans 3:10 (NLT)

(Righteous equals perfect.) No matter how much I strive for perfection, it's not going to happen. And, when I strive for perfection, I set myself up as an idol. Again, flashing back to Sunday school:

> You shall have no other gods before me.
>
> Exodus 20:3 (NIV)

Notice the "g" in "gods" is a lowercase "g." There is only one true God (capital "G"). Any other god (lowercase "g") is a cheap imitation, an idol. He is the real deal, and He shares His throne with nobody (including yours truly).

> Trust in the Lord with all your heart and *lean not on your own understanding*; in all your ways submit to Him and He will make your paths straight.
>
> Proverbs 3:5–6 (NIV, author's italics)

I just looked up The Message Version of Proverbs 3:5–6 and found it quite relevant to my superpower:

> Trust God from the bottom of your heart; don't try to figure out everything on your own. Listen for God's voice in everything you do, everywhere you go;
> he's the one who will keep you on track.
>
> Proverbs 3:5–6 (MSG)

Wow! I am learning as I am writing!

Let's take this a step further. I pull out my Jeremiah Study Bible[4] and dig deeper. It truly is a unique study Bible. My husband and I flew to New York City to the launch of Dr. Jeremiah's new Bible at Madison Square Garden. Throughout his Bible, which is the New King James Version, Dr. Jeremiah penned his own study notes and included his sermon notes, as well. I peeked in to see what he had to say about Proverbs 3:5–6. In paraphrase, he basically said that we need to be walking in obedience in order to activate God's promises for our lives.

Further, if we try to figure things out on our own, we are actually walking in disobedience. That makes perfect sense to me, although I often find it difficult to do. This Type-A go-girl likes to get ahead of God's plan by trying to figure things out for herself.

There is a lot to unpack there. Just as Jesus revealed to me in my quiet time, trying to figure everything out is idolatry. I am relying on myself versus relying totally and completely on Him. Having God direct our paths is a good thing, right? Have you seen that cartoon of a man telling a story and a woman telling the same story? The bubble over the man's head shows a direct route, straight to the bottom line. The bubble over the woman's head shows a more circuitous route that resembles a plate of spaghetti. I think that is what my path must look like when I try to figure things out versus letting God direct my path. My life has been a plate of spaghetti because trying to figure things out on my own was a total disregard for His perfect will.

I like the truth that God's will is activated in our lives when we obey. I think my life script can still look like spaghetti if I do not practice *immediate* obedience. (Lack of immediate obedience has been equated to disobedience in the Bible. Think Jonah.) I say that because I often find myself taking the long route (forty years wandering in the desert) versus the direct route because I am not immediately obedient. I get around to being obedient, but only after I have taken many wrong turns along the way. Immediate obedience is a more direct route to making my path straight. God said it in His Word (Proverbs 3:5–6), but my superpower takes over. I need to ditch that superpower. I am made in the image of God (*imago Dei*), but that does not mean that I have to have it all figured out.

Chapter 10

4-H

> I am the good shepherd. The good shepherd lays
> down his life for the sheep.
>
> John 10:11 (NIV)

Is 4-H still a thing? For many years, it was a big thing for me. My mom put my brother and I in 4-H not only to learn to do neat things, but 4-H also had a strong emphasis on values, as evidenced by the 4-H pledge (which I still remember to this day):

> I pledge my head to clearer thinking,
> My heart to greater loyalty.
> My hands to larger service.
> And my health to better living.
> For my club, my community, my country and
> my world.[5]

Wouldn't this country be a better place if we all lived up to the ideals described in the 4-H pledge?

4-H was helpful for me in coming out of my introverted shell and feelings of unworthiness. (Although those feelings would become a lifelong struggle.) But it was a start. We began early on to do public speaking and were entered into public speaking contests beginning in about the fifth grade. I did well at public speaking because I possessed the spiritual gift of gab. (That spiritual gift often landed me in the corner, though.)

In 4-H, you pick different projects that you want to work on throughout the year, and you keep records of each project in your record book. The Super Bowl for a 4-Her is the county fair. There, you "show" your projects and receive awards for your achievements. I chose many projects throughout the years, including art, leathercraft, photography, gardening, and raising rabbits and sheep.

Raising sheep was probably the most rewarding and hardest project I ever chose. We bought baby lambs and raised them to sell at the county fair. My brother named his lamb Smokey, and I named my lamb Jerry. Just like in the Bible, our lambs knew our voices, and we knew theirs. It is interesting that when I heard one bleating, I knew which lamb it was. (A bleat is a weak cry of a lamb or calf.) My brother and I would put leashes on our lambs and walk them around the neighborhood like dogs. We fed them, combed their hair, bathed them, dipped them for ticks, etc. We spent so much time with them that they thought they were our dogs.

One morning, my brother ran into the house and yelled at Mom to keep me in the house. He told my dad to grab his gun and come out to the sheep pen. Stray dogs had gotten in the sheep pen overnight and literally eaten our sheep alive. Sheep are extremely meek and mild animals and not capable of defending themselves. The sheep had to be euthanized, which was a hard pill for a twelve-year-old to swallow. My grandfather was a butcher by trade, so he agreed to butcher the sheep and give (supposedly) the meat to the poor.

I have an awesome brother. Six months after the sheep incident, we were sitting at the table eating dinner when my brother spoke up and said, "Please pass Jerry!" At that, my dad popped him on the back of the head, and I jumped up and ran from the table, crying hysterically. Needless to say, to this day, I do not eat mutton!

When I read about Jesus being the Good Shepherd in the Bible, I can sort of relate. After all, I was a kind of shepherdess for a little while. As I said before, I knew my lamb's voice, and he knew mine.

In the book of John, Jesus tells us that He is the Good Shepherd.

> I am the good shepherd; I know my sheep and my sheep know me—just as the Father knows me and I know the Father—and I lay down my life for the sheep.
>
> John 10:14–15 (NIV)

John takes it a step further in verse 27 and says,

> My sheep listen to my voice; I know them, and they follow me.
>
> John 10:27 (NIV)

Do you know how sheep recognize the voice of their shepherd? They spend time with the shepherd. After raising sheep, this concept makes so much sense to me. Jerry knew me, and he knew my voice because we spent a lot of time together. I am learning to recognize the voice of my Good Shepherd because I spend time with Him. I wish I could say that I spent my whole life getting to know the Good Shepherd and recognizing His voice, but that would be a lie. There was about a ten-year period in my thirties when I was a wandering, lost sheep, "looking for love in all the wrong places."

This is where another illustration in the Bible about the Good Shepherd is so relevant to my life.

> Suppose one of you has a hundred sheep and loses one of them. Doesn't he leave the ninety-nine in the open country and go after the lost sheep until he finds it? And when he finds it, he joyfully puts it on his shoulders and goes home. Then he calls his friends and neighbors together and says, "Rejoice with me; I have found my lost sheep." I tell you that in the same way there will be more rejoicing in heaven over one sinner who repents than over ninety-nine righteous persons who do not need to repent.
>
> Luke 15:4–7 (NIV)

I was that lost sheep. Jesus came after me. He relentlessly pursued me. He put me over His shoulders and carried me home. Every morning in my quiet time, I praise God because He rescued me. He redeemed me. He restored me. He recreated me. He renamed me.

I was made in the image of God (*imago Dei*)…of course, He would come after me! Friend, spend time with the Good Shepherd, and get to know His voice!

Chapter 11

Label Maker

> Put on the full armor of God, so that you can take your stand against the devil's schemes.
>
> Ephesians 6:11 (NIV)

    I was strolling through the office supplies aisle at Walmart yesterday, looking for a 2024 calendar. Can I tell you, the OCD in me loves office supplies? Office Depot is my happy place. Pens, highlighters, sticky notes, journals, oh my! At Walmart, I came across a shelf full of label makers. My heart began to race! Oh, what I could do with a label maker! I began to fantasize about labeling my entire pantry. Then, in my mind, I moved on to my office. *I could be uber-organized if I invested in a label maker.* My husband would have made such fun of me because labels state the obvious. Labels in my pantry might read "flour," "sugar," "crackers," etc. You get the picture. I did not leave Walmart with a label maker because I knew that I would be feeding the beast and wasting precious time labeling everything that did not move.

    Do labels about people state the obvious? What false labels do I carry about myself? What false labels do you carry? I travel for work, so I listen to a lot of podcasts. I am not sure who said this, and it may be a bit paraphrased,

Imago Dei

but it really resonated with me: "For every label the Enemy places on me, Jesus gives me a new name."

"Samaritan" was a label used in the Bible. Samaritans were considered "less than," a label. Samaritans were considered "half-breeds" (another label) because they were half Jewish and half Assyrian. They only honored the first five books of the Bible (the Pentateuch), so they were outcasts in Israel. Many Jews avoided traveling through Samaria and instead would take the long way around Samaria to avoid contact with the "less than." But not Jesus. He came to save *all*, including Samaritans.

John 4 tells the story of Jesus traveling through Samaria, which was on His route from Judea to Galilee. Again, that was not the custom in those days. Most of the Galilean Jews would have taken a more circuitous route, avoiding Samaria altogether. Jesus stopped around noon at Jacob's well to rest and refresh. A Samaritan woman came to the well to get some water, and Jesus asked her if she would give Him a drink. This was a really, really big deal. In the culture at that time, the only thing lower than being a female was to be a Samaritan female.

> The Samaritan woman said to him, "You are a Jew and I am a Samaritan woman. How can you ask me for a drink?" (For Jews do not associate with Samaritans.)
>
> John 4:9 (NIV)

I am sure when she walked up to Jesus, she did not make eye contact with Him. She probably had her gaze lowered and was going to get her water as quickly and efficiently as she could and get gone.

But. Jesus. Spoke.

When Jesus spoke to her, many new labels were communicated to her. The first label Jesus communicated to her was, "I see you." She was seen. She was a woman. She was a Samaritan. Yet, she was seen. She would later find out that she was not seen by any old traveler on the road to Galilee. She was seen by the Savior of the world.

Another new label that Jesus gave her was that she was worthy. She was worthy of His time. She was worthy of His words. She was worthy of His love. She was worthy enough to be the *first* person to whom Jesus would reveal His true identity...as the Messiah.

Jesus gave her the label "clean." Jesus came to the well with nothing to dip in the well and nothing to drink out of. So, when He asked her to give Him a drink, He intended to drink after her. Her response in verse 11 was that of a confused Samaritan woman who was used to being labeled as unclean.

> "Sir," the woman said, "You have nothing to draw with and the well is deep."
>
> John 4:11a (NIV)

> Jesus answered, "Everyone who drinks this water will be thirsty again, but whoever drinks the water I give them will never thirst. Indeed, the water I give them will become in them a spring of water welling up to eternal life."
>
> John 4:13–14 (NIV)

At His words, the woman asked Jesus to give her that living water so that she would never thirst again. Jesus told her to first go and get her husband and then come back. She told Him that she didn't have a husband. Jesus told her that she was right; she didn't presently have a husband. She had five husbands, and right then, she was just living with a guy.

The label the Samaritan woman had taken upon herself (and the label the community had probably given her) was "shame." Her community said, "Shame on you." But Jesus said, "Shame off you." Because He is the living water. He is the Messiah.

The story ends with Jesus revealing to her that He is the Messiah.

> The woman said, "I know that Messiah" (called Christ) "is coming. When he comes, he will explain everything to us."
> Then Jesus declared, "I, the one speaking to you—I am he."
>
> John 4:25–26 (NIV)

The story ends there, and we don't exactly know if she accepted Jesus as her Messiah or not. (Although she did say she wanted the living water.) But I bet she did. He gave her many new labels. He took the shame off her. He saw her and sat with her in her shame and gave her hope (living water) and a new name. She was able to raise her gaze to the One who offered her redemption and eternal life.

I am the woman at the well. I have made some poor decisions that brought shame to myself and to my children. I knowingly and willingly wandered off like a lost sheep. I knew the truth, yet I still wandered. Jesus saw me. He sat with me in my shame. He asked me for a drink of water. I chose His living water. He raised my gaze.

> Therefore, if anyone is in Christ, the new creation has come: the old has gone, the new is here!
>
> 2 Corinthians 5:17 (NIV)

I saw a post on Facebook the other day that said, "It wasn't water that Jesus came for; it was me!" Now, I have a new label...redeemed. I am *imago Dei*. He made me in His image, and He died to complete the "Great Exchange." His righteousness for my sin. His righteousness for your sin.

Chapter 12

Backpacking

> My son, give me your heart, and let your eyes delight in my ways.
>
> Proverbs 23:26 (NIV)

I was raised in the Sangre de Cristo Mountains of northern New Mexico, and I have lived my entire adult life in the foothills of the Ozark Mountains in Arkansas. I love the mountains, and I love the outdoors. I love to marvel at the beauty of His creation. That's why I often refer to Jesus as my "Creator Redeemer."

I am an avid backpacker, but not the kind of backpacker that you might think. Let me explain. Several years ago, while I was a single mom navigating raising two boys on my own, I was asked to teach a Sunday school class for other single moms. We named ourselves "Balancing Act" because it accurately reflected our current season of life.

One Sunday morning, I came into class with a backpack on my back. (Little did the class know, it was full of bricks.) I passed the backpack around and had everybody try it on to see how heavy it was. Then I proceeded to put it on my back and carry it around the whole time I was teaching about my journey as a backpacker.

When I say I am an avid backpacker, that is an understatement. I am an aficionado at carrying my spiritual backpack...everywhere I go. One of the lies that Satan the Deceiver told me as a single mother was that I was alone in the journey and that I had to do everything on my own. I would pray about something and lay my backpack at the foot of the cross; then, I would pick it up again...usually in record time. Over the years, my backpacking would become more and more. I would lay the burden down, only to pick it up again moments later. I still suffer from the disease of backpacking today, only now to a lesser extent. My backpack has become lighter as I have begun to learn how to lay my burdens down. I hope to one day be fully rid of my backpack.

My constant backpacking tells me an unhappy truth about myself...I have trust issues. I must think that the God of the Universe, my Creator Redeemer, can't handle whatever I am going through. Ouch! But that is the case, isn't it? If I keep surrendering my backpack to Him just to pick it up moments later, I must not trust Him. I say I trust Him, but do I really? Yikes!

I used to seriously dislike the old hymn "I Surrender All." It used to bother me and occasionally still does, for a good reason. "Surrender" is often a dirty word to me.

> All to Jesus I surrender,
> All to Him I freely give.
> I will ever love and trust Him
> In His presence daily live.
> I surrender all.
> I surrender all.
> All to Thee my blessed Savior,

Imago Dei

> I surrender all.[6]

It's convicting, isn't it? Jesus wants me to surrender. He wants me to lay my burdens down. He can handle it. I can trust Him with what I care about. He didn't create me in His image (*imago Dei*) to struggle with a backpack. He created me for an abundant life!

> The thief comes except to steal, and to kill, and to destroy. I have come that they may have life, and that they may have it more abundantly.
>
> John 10:10 (NKJV)

Pay attention to words and phrases that are repeated in the Bible because God wants us to hear Him! He repeats the word "abundant" again in Ephesians 3:20a (NKJV):

> Now to Him who is able to do exceedingly abundantly above all that we ask or think…

He is able. Lay that backpack down.

In Matthew, Jesus tells His weary children to lay their burdens down and let Him pick them up and carry them.

> Come to me, all you who are weary and burdened, and I will give you rest. Take my yoke upon you and learn from me, for I am gentle and humble in heart, and you will find rest for your souls. For my yoke is easy and my burden is light.
>
> Matthew 11:28–30 (NIV)

We know that a yoke is a wooden collar that is placed

over two animals and then attached to a plow or cart. So... putting on a yoke sounds like work (like carrying a backpack!) I wondered about that, so I whipped out my Jeremiah Study Bible[7] to see what he had to say about it in his notes. Again, in paraphrase, Dr. Jeremiah said that taking that yoke was much like walking in another person's steps and learning from them. In today's terms, it's sort of like a mentoring relationship. Walking in step with Jesus relieves stress. I like that. If I follow Him, walk in His footsteps, and give Him my backpack, then I will live a life free of (self-imposed) stress.

Let's end this backpacking adventure with The Message Version of Matthew 11:28–30. It's pretty refreshing:

> Are you tired? Worn out? Burned out on religion? Come to me. Get away with me and you'll recover your life. I'll show you how to take a real rest. Walk with me and work with me— watch how I do it. Learn the unforced rhythms of grace. I won't lay anything heavy or ill-fitting on you. Keep company with me and you'll learn to live freely and lightly.
>
> Matthew 11:28–30 (MSG)

Unforced rhythms of grace, I like that! We can live freely and lightly because we are His image bearers...*imago Dei*.

Chapter 13

The Kid's Table

As they sat down to eat, he took the bread and
blessed it. Then he broke it and gave it to them.

Luke 24:30 (NLT)

We used to have family reunions twice a year on my mom's side of the family, at Thanksgiving and again on Memorial Day. As a kid, I thought it was boring sitting around and watching the elders play dominoes and tell the same stories year after year. We had a pretty decent-sized family that consisted of a lot of folks who were my grandparents' age and not very many cousins my age. As in many families in the '60s and '70s, the younger attendees were relegated to the kids' table during meals. We were usually a bit rowdy and loud at the kids' table. We often got "the eye," which meant "we better settle down."

Our family had a strong bond of Christian faith, which meant we prayed before every meal. At one particular family reunion, my great-uncle Joe was asked to pray. (He was often asked to bless our meal because he was the most "qualified," being a Baptist preacher.) The problem that year was that Uncle Joe was a bit windy in his prayer. The preparations for the meal had taken a bit longer than anticipated, and being the "strapping" young girl that I was, my internal dinner bell had rung about an hour previous. During Uncle Joe's voracious prayer, I began to "eye" the stuffed celery. My pudgy little hand began to make its way over to the lovely display of celery piled high, just waiting for me to dive in. I snuck a celery stick, and the minute Uncle Joe said amen, I bit into that crunchy piece of deliciousness. *Crunch!* Everybody turned and looked at me, including my mother. There was that "eye." I knew some unpleasantness was coming my way. Mom jumped up from the adult table, marched over to the kids' table, where I was ruminating on my stuffed celery stick, and snatched me up in one fell swoop. I was up from the table and on the back porch in record time. Let's just say my lunch was over, my backside was sore, and I was made to apologize to old Uncle Joe for the disrespect that I had shown him and his prayer…and Jesus.

That probably was not the only mayhem that I got into at the kids' table, but it was the most memorable. Did you ever have to sit at the kids' table at family gatherings? In my Bible study this week, I have been reading a lot about the table that Jesus invites us to sit at with Him. His table is *big*. His table is for *all*. There is no kids' table. I get to sit at His table with Him!

I never realized just how much there is in the Bible about the significance of the table. Think about how many times you see in Jesus's ministry that He broke bread with others around a table. The table of fellowship was huge in His ministry, and it was recorded over and over again in the gospel that He broke bread with sinners and tax collectors. (A tax collector was considered the lowest of the lows in biblical times.) There was no "kids' table." Jesus did not just sit with the "pretty" or "holy" people. The invitation to sit at Jesus's table was open to *all*…as it still is today.

I am currently enjoying Kristi McLelland's Bible study

IMAGO DEI

called *The Gospel on the Ground*,[8] which is a study of the book of Acts. She gives many examples of the significance of the "table of fellowship" to early believers as a tool in spreading the gospel of Jesus Christ. She references the table as the "Table of Welcome" and talks about the importance of table fellowship. Kristi talks about the fact that in biblical times, who you ate with said a lot about who you were. In those days, a person was known more by whom they broke bread with than they were by their profession. (Reminder: Jesus broke bread with folks who were considered "less than.") She also talked about the fact that if you were invited to somebody's table, it was more than just an invitation to eat. It was more like an invitation to be part of the family. The book of Acts is the account of the explosion of the gospel. Home churches began to spring up as believers gathered around tables of fellowship and broke bread together. The table of fellowship was used in those days to invite others to become a member of the family of God.

> They devoted themselves to the apostles' teaching and to fellowship, to the *breaking of bread* and to prayer. Everyone was filled with awe at the many wonders and signs performed by the apostles. All the believers were together and had everything in common. They sold property and possessions to give to anyone who had need. Every day they continued to meet together in the temple courts. They *broke bread in their homes* and ate together with glad and sincere hearts, praising God and enjoying the favor of all the people. And the Lord added to their number daily those who were being saved.
>
> Acts 2:42–47 (NIV, author's italics)

Every Baptist church that I have ever attended had

a Sunday school class called "Koinonia." *Koinonia* is a Greek term that translates as "fellowship." It literally means to "share things together." *Koinonia* was the tool that the early believers used to spread the gospel "in Jerusalem, and in all Judea and Samaria, and to the ends of the earth" (Acts 1:8b, NIV).

Heaven is often referred to as the "Banquet Table." I do love to eat, so naturally, I can relate to the analogy that heaven is a banquet table. I will take that one step further... heaven is like a banquet table with all your favorite things, and *there are no calories*! In all seriousness, a banquet table is *big*. The banquet table is *special*. There is room for *everybody* (who has accepted Jesus's open invitation of eternal life) to the wedding supper of the Lamb (His banquet table). John, in the book of Revelation, tells us about the wedding supper of the Lamb, when Christ and His bride (the church) are reunited. (Cue: "Reunited" by Peaches and Herb, circa 1978—you millennials might need to Google that one.)

> Then I heard what sounded like a great multitude, like the roar of rushing waters and like loud peals of thunder, shouting:
> "Hallelujah!
> For our Lord God Almighty reigns.
> Let us rejoice and be glad and give Him glory!
> For the *wedding* of the Lamb has come,
> and His *bride* has made herself ready.
> Fine linen, bright and clean, was given her to wear."
> (Fine linen stands for the righteous acts of God's holy people.)
> Then the angel said to me, "Write this: Blessed are those who are invited to the wedding supper of the Lamb!" And he added, "These are the true words of God."
>
> Revelation 19:6–9 (NIV, author's italics)

In Kristi's Bible study, she talked about the fact that when we eat together, it's really a practice session for the wedding supper of the Lamb. I like that! A thought…Jesus will do some of His best work around my dining table. I need to get busy inviting others to my table of fellowship.

Because we are all made in the image of God (*imago Dei*), we get to sit at Jesus's table. We don't have to get "all cleaned up," and there is no kids' table.

CHAPTER 14

Walker, Texas Ranger

> Wait for the Lord; be strong, and let your heart
> take courage; wait for the Lord!
>
> Psalm 27:14 (ESV)

My boys stayed with my parents during the summer for many years. They had a routine. They would golf with my parents in the morning until lunchtime. Then they would eat. Then, they would help my dad with chores or explore their mini farm. In the afternoon, they would come in and watch TV. They never wanted me to pick them up before 4:00 because they would watch back-to-back episodes of *Walker, Texas Ranger* that ended at 4:00. Chuck Norris played Cordell Walker, a Texas Ranger, highly skilled in kicking in doors, hand-to-hand combat, and creative crime solving.

I have watched many episodes over the years, and I am happy to report that *I am Chuck Norris*. "Did I read that right?" (You might be wondering.) The answer is a resounding, "Yes, you did." What Chuck Norris (aka *Walker, Texas Ranger*) was really good at was kicking in doors. He rarely knocked. He rarely announced his presence. He probably never had search warrants, as is required in today's police TV shows. He would rear back, give a full frontal kick, and the door would go crashing in.

I am a door kicker...not in the literal sense like Chuck, but in the spiritual sense. And...I am really efficient at it. Satan tells us that we need to be self-sufficient. Satan tells us that if we want to get anything done, we need to do it ourselves and do it *now*. He wants us to kick that door in because he knows if we go in before God, we are going to fail. He doesn't want us to seek God. He doesn't want us to wait for God's perfect timing. He doesn't want us to allow God to go before us. He wants us to charge right up, kick that door open, and do it (whatever "it" may be) ourselves.

The problem I have encountered with being a Chuck Norris door kicker is it usually ends in mayhem. You've seen those mayhem commercials, right? That is what I usually look like (spiritually) after I have kicked the door open and made my own way.

Verses like Psalm 46:10 (NLT), "Be still, and know that I am God..." are hard for me because I like to charge full steam ahead. If I were guessing, that verse is probably hard for you, as well. That's because Satan likes to get in our heads and tell us that we can do it on our own. That's kind of interesting. Satan, the Deceiver, contradicts himself a lot. (You'll never see God contradict Himself.) What I mean about Satan contradicting himself is this: on the one hand, he tells us that we are unworthy, we are failures, and we can't do anything.

On the other hand, he tells us that we are strong and independent and we don't need anybody's help. See what I mean? Satan is not only the author of lies, but he's also the ringmaster of confusion.

There are many examples in the Bible of Satan telling people to go out ahead of God and do their own thing. There are also many examples of calamity ensuing and consequences being paid when God's kids kicked in the door and did things on their own. The first example is right up front in the Bible, Genesis Chapter 3, verses 1–7 (NLT): The Fall.

> The serpent was the shrewdest of all the wild animals the Lord God had made. One day he asked the woman, "Did God really say you must not eat the fruit from any of the trees in the garden?"
>
> "Of course we may eat fruit from the trees in the garden," the woman replied. "It's only the fruit from the tree in the middle of the garden that we are not allowed to eat. God said, 'You must not eat it or even touch it; if you do, you will die.'
>
> "You won't die!" the serpent replied to the woman. "God knows that your eyes will be opened as soon as you eat it, and you will be like God knowing both good and evil."
>
> The woman was convinced. She saw that the tree was beautiful and its fruit looked delicious, and she wanted the wisdom it would give her. So she took some of the fruit and ate it. Then she gave some to her husband, who was with her, and he ate it, too. At that moment their eyes were opened, and they suddenly felt shame at their nakedness. So they sewed fig leaves together to cover themselves.
>
> Genesis 3:1–7 (NLT)

What if Eve had taken the time to realize whose voice was coming out of the serpent? What if Eve had gone to God (with whom she had a direct line) and told Him what the serpent had said and asked Him what she should do? What if she had walked away? What if…? But no, her acquiescence to the serpent changed the course of all of humanity. And...misery loves company, right? She dragged Adam into the whole disobedience thing. Sin entered the world, and separation from God began. All because Eve *did not wait on God* and listened to the lies of the enemy instead.

An interesting side note: we tend to assume that the fruit from the tree was an apple, right? That's what all the TV shows, commercials, and artwork have depicted. Again, as I was watching the *Gospel on the Ground*[9] Bible study video by Kristi McLelland, I was fascinated by an interesting observation that she made. She said she found it curious that after Adam and Eve ate the fruit, they covered themselves with *fig* leaves. (Obviously, fig trees must have been in close proximity.) She then goes on to point out that the only tree that Jesus ever cursed was a *fig* tree (Mark 11:12–25). Hmmm, now that is interesting. When we get to heaven, we'll have to ask Eve two questions. The first one will be, "What were you thinking?" The second question will be, "What kind of fruit was it?"

We've already talked about another example of getting ahead of God and kicking open the door of opportunity when Sarai encouraged Abram to lie with her servant, Hagar, to bear him a son. The consequences of her refusal to wait for God (impatience) and handle things on her own resulted in generational consequences.

Joseph...now there's a great example of patience in the process. Let's review the story (Genesis 37–50) in a Reader's Digest Condensed version. Here we go: Joseph was more loved by his father (Jacob) than his brothers were. Because of that great love, his dad made him a special coat. The brothers did not appreciate the favoritism their father showed Joseph. Now, Joseph was a dreamer and also had the God-given ability to interpret dreams. They really, really did not appreciate Joseph sharing his dream that basically said they would someday bow down to him. So, they sold Joseph, the dreamer, into slavery.

The Lord was with Joseph and granted him favor. He was second only to Potiphar. Chapter 39 says that Joseph was a looker, and Potipher's wife took a shine to him. She kept trying to get Joseph to be her "special friend," but Joseph, being an honorable man, kept deflecting her flirtations. Joseph fled from her, and she grabbed his special coat and used it as evidence that Joseph had been inappropriate with her. Off to jail, Joseph went, but the Lord continued to be with him, even in jail. God gave Joseph success in everything he did, and he rose in favor (jail cred). This is where his dreamy talent came into play. He was able to interpret the dreams of fellow prisoners and was quite accurate. He asked the cupbearer, for whom he had accurately interpreted his dream, to remember him when he was again in the presence of the king. The cupbearer promised he would. But did he? Ummm...no.

Joseph remained faithful. He didn't whine or complain. He didn't try to manipulate his way out of jail. Remember, he had the favor of those in charge of his incarceration (jail cred) and probably could have set the wheels in motion for his return to society. Nope...he waited. And waited. For two full years, he waited and trusted God.

Then, the pharaoh had a dream, and only Joseph could provide the correct interpretation. Why? Because he had God-given ability and he was faithful to God. You know how the story ends. Joseph foretells seven years of prosperity followed by seven years of famine. God elevates Joseph to be over all of Egypt, and he begins to store up grain in anticipation of the famine. The story ends with Joseph saving the lives not only of Egypt but of his family. Joseph *waited* on God for justice. Joseph *waited* on God for restoration. Joseph *waited* on God for favor. Joseph *waited* to be used by God. Some of the most famous words in the Bible came from Joseph toward the end of Genesis:

> You intended to harm me, but God intended it
> for good to accomplish what is now being done,
> the saving of many lives.

Genesis 50:20 (NIV)

I love it when the good guys win! I love it when the Enemy's evil plans are thwarted! I love it when God gives us examples in His Word to show us that listening to His voice is far more profitable than listening to the voice of the Enemy. Satan probably told Joseph to kick in that door of opportunity. God probably told him, "*Wait.* I have a plan."

That is a good word for us today. There is no need to be Chuck Norris door kickers. *Wait* on God, praise Him in the hallway, and *wait* for Him to open that door. We are *imago Dei*, and He won't leave us in the hallway forever.

Chapter 15

DQd

> But I trust that you will know that we are not disqualified.
>
> 2 Corinthians 13:6 (NKJV)

No, "DQ" does not stand for Dairy Queen, although that is my favorite "DQ." DQ stands for disqualified, and it's a title (from the Enemy) that I have taken on for a very long time.

In 2020, a US female sprinter became one of the fastest women of all time in the 100-meter dash. She was expected to bring home the gold from the Tokyo Olympics that summer. But…she was never allowed to run the 100 meters at the Olympics because she had tested positive for a banned substance during the Olympic time trials. Disqualified.

Disqualification is a hard thing. It's especially hard when a disqualification is self-inflicted. It is usually the result of a personal decision or action, and there is always a cost. Webster defines "disqualified" as "to make ineligible for a prize or for further competition because of violations of the rules."[10]

The Enemy gave me the title of "disqualified" many years ago, and I bought into that lie. As I have told you before, we make decisions based on how we see ourselves. I made two bad marriage decisions in my life based on the labels (lies) that the Enemy placed on me. He told me I was unattractive. He told me I was unlovable. He told me I was unworthy. The heart of a third-grade little girl who believed the Enemy and marriage and divorce decisions were made later in life because of my belief in those lies. I believed the lie that "I would be better off being a single parent" and chose divorce. Then, less than a year later, I believed the lie that "I was a nobody if I didn't have somebody" and made a marriage decision that was far less than stellar.

I like Webster's definition of "disqualified" because that is exactly how I have felt: "to make ineligible for a prize…because of violations of the rules." I had violated God's rules for marriage. God put rules in place for my own good. Let me repeat that: God put rules in place for my own good. Rules may seem restrictive or even harsh. But ultimately, they *are* for our own good. You've heard the phrase, "Hindsight is 20/20." That is so true! When looking in the rearview mirror of my life, I can see the choices that I made and the resulting consequences that I (and my boys) suffered. What is so hard to deal with is that those were choices that I made. I did it to myself. I knowingly (and willingly) walked away from the Truth and decided that I could handle things on my own.

So, where does the label "disqualified" come into play? I have been a writer and a communicator all my life. I have journaled. I have written essays. I have blogged. I have taught Bible studies. I have a love for sharing "the hope that is within me." But I made a couple of devastating life choices, and the Enemy told me that I could not make a difference in the lives of other women because of my missteps (sin). Disqualified. The big DQ.

I have come to realize something important: what God

says about me is true. The labels that God puts on me are real. God's plan for me is good. God is in the restoration business, and I am living proof that what the Enemy intended for evil, God intended for good. My mistakes (sin) do not define me, nor do they define my future. God and His forgiveness are bigger than my sin. The blood that Jesus shed to cover my sin *is enough*! And...He can still use me!

The apostle Paul messed up. Like, he messed up *big time*. He was a zealous persecutor of Christians. He sought them out and murdered them for their belief in God. Till one day, on that road to Damascus, God got Paul's attention:

> Meanwhile, Saul was still breathing out murderous threats against the Lord's disciples. He went to the high priest and asked him for letters to the synagogues in Damascus, so that if he found any there who belonged to the Way, whether men or women, he might take them as prisoners to Jerusalem. As he neared Damascus on his journey, suddenly a light from heaven flashed around him. He fell to the ground and heard a voice say to him, "Saul, Saul, why do you persecute me?"
>
> "Who are you, Lord?" Saul asked.
>
> "I am Jesus, who you are persecuting," he replied. "Now get up and go into the city, and you will be told what you must do."
>
> The men traveling with Saul stood there speechless; they heard the sound but did not see anyone. Saul got up from the ground, but when he opened his eyes he could see nothing. So they led him by the hand into Damascus. For three days he was blind and did not eat or drink anything.
>
> Acts 9:1–9 (NIV)

Ananias was a disciple who lived in Damascus. God called out to Ananias and told him to go to a certain place where he would find Saul and restore his sight. Ananias didn't really dig the idea of looking Saul (soon to be called Paul) up, but nonetheless, he was obedient.

> But the Lord said to Ananias, "Go! This man is my chosen instrument to proclaim my name to the Gentiles and their kings and to the people of Israel."
>
> Acts 9:15 (NIV)

The rest, you could say, is history. If anybody deserved to be "DQd," it was Paul. Yet, God used him to build His church. He was the Billy Graham of the early church.

> Then Ananias went to the house and entered it. Placing his hands on Saul, he said, "Brother Saul, the Lord—Jesus, who appeared to you on the road as you were coming here—has sent me so that you may see again and be filled with the Holy Spirit." Immediately, something like scales fell from Saul's eyes, and he could see again. He got up and was baptized, and after taking some food, he regained his strength.
>
> Saul spent several days with the disciples in Damascus. At once he began to preach in the synagogues that Jesus is the Son of God. All those who heard him were astonished and asked, "Isn't he the man who raised havoc in Jerusalem among those who call on this name? And hasn't he come here to take them as prisoners to the chief priests?" Yet Saul grew more and more powerful and baffled the Jews living in Damascus by proving that Jesus is the Messiah.
>
> Acts 9:17–22 (NIV)

> Then the church throughout Judea, Galilee and Samaria enjoyed a time of peace and was strengthened. Living in the fear of the Lord and encouraged by the Holy Spirit, it increased in numbers.
>
> Acts 9:31 (NIV)

Wow! What Satan intended for evil (the killing of believers), God truly intended for good (the building up of His church)! God can truly make beauty from ashes. This is my story. He took the ashes of my life, cleaned it up, and turned it around. He can do that for you, too. It's a promise in His Word:

> And provide for those who grieve in Zion—to bestow on them a crown of *beauty* instead of ashes, the oil of *joy* instead of mourning, and a garment of *praise* instead of despair. They will be called oaks of righteousness, a planting of the Lord for the display of his splendor.
>
> Isaiah 61:3 (NIV, author's italics)

I love the very last part: "A planting of the Lord for the display of his splendor." He will use our collective stories for His glory. How awesome is that?

So, we are *not* disqualified. He will use our stories for His glory. Put on your garment of praise, for you are *imago Dei*...made in His image for Him to display His splendor!

Chapter 16

Two Fish Sandwiches

> And God is able to make all grace abound toward you, that you, always having all sufficiency in all things, may have an abundance for every good work.
>
> 2 Corinthians 9:8 (NKJV)

Have you ever felt like you weren't "enough"? That is one of Satan's favorite lies. He knows the Scripture just as well as we do, yet he chooses to forget the promise in Philippians 4:13 that we can do *all* things because He (Jesus) gives us the strength and ability to do so. Sometimes, I forget that verse, too. I tell myself that "I can't," or "I'm not strong enough," or "I'm not smart enough," or just plain, "I'm not enough." But God, in His Word, tells me a different story. He tells me that I can do *all* things because of Him. Period. *All* things. Not some things. Not a few things...*all* things.

But I think there is a condition to *all* things. The condition is found back in John 15, in the analogy of the Vine and the branches. John 15 tells us:

> I am the vine; you are the branches. If you remain in me and I in you, you will bare much

fruit; apart from me you can do nothing.

John 15:5 (NIV)

If He is going to give me the strength to do *all* things, then I must first be connected to Him (the Vine), the source of my power. After all, you can't turn on a lamp if it is not connected to the power source, right?

Once in a great while, I enjoy a McDonald's Filet-O-Fish Sandwich without the tartar sauce. I also enjoy the story of the fish sandwiches in the Bible. In Mark 6, we learn the story of Jesus feeding the 5,000. The number was actually greater than that because the last line in the story tells us that Jesus fed 5,000 *men* that day. The headcount did not include the women and the children. I think the count was probably more along the lines of 15,000 to 20,000. That's a big banquet to prepare and serve. (Miracle loading.)

> The apostles then rendezvoused with Jesus and reported on all that they had done and taught. Jesus said, "Come off by yourselves; let's take a break and get a little rest." For there was constant coming and going. They didn't even have time to eat.
>
> So, they got in the boat and went off to a remote place by themselves. Someone saw them going and the word got around. From the surrounding towns people went out on foot, running, and got there ahead of them. When Jesus arrived, he saw this huge crowd. At the sight of them, his heart broke—like sheep with no shepherd they were. He went right to work teaching them.
>
> When his disciples thought this had gone on long enough—it was now quite late in the day—

> they interrupted: "We are a long way out in the country, and it's very late. Pronounce a benediction and send those folks off so they can get some supper."
>
> Mark 6:30–36 (MSG)

The disciples had been hard at work, teaching, and traveling, so much so that they hadn't even had time to eat lunch. If the disciples were anything like me, they probably were becoming a little bit hangry. Jesus, with His eyes of compassion, invited them to get alone with Him and rest. That's a good word for me when presented with an obstacle or an opportunity...get away with Jesus. My instinct tells me to jump right in and make things happen, but I know that without Him, I can do nothing (John 15:5). So first, I need to get alone with Jesus, rest (be still), and pray.

A huge crowd had formed, and Jesus saw His opportunity for a divine appointment, the feeding of their souls. In His eyes, they were like sheep without a shepherd. His heart broke for them, and He got right to work, teaching and healing the crowd until late. The disciples were probably still very hungry, and it was getting late, so they interrupted Jesus. Who does that? Who walks up to the King of kings and gives Him the signal to wrap it up? Well, the disciples did. They told Jesus to cut it short; it was getting late, and the people needed to go home so they could eat. What do you think Jesus's response was?

> Jesus said, "You do it. Fix supper for them."
> They replied, "Are you serious? You want us to go spend a fortune on food for their supper?"
> But he was quite serious. "How many loaves of bread do you have? Take an inventory."
> That didn't take long. "Five," they said, "plus

two fish."

Mark 6:37–38 (MSG)

The second thing this story tells me to do when I am dealing with an obstacle or an opportunity is to take inventory. I need to take stock of the resources that I have at my disposal. The disciples quickly took stock of what the crowd had on hand and reported back. It didn't take long because there wasn't much inventory. The account in the Gospel of John says that a young boy had just enough for a couple of fish sandwiches (hold the tartar sauce.) Side note: that boy had the *best* mama of the whole crowd because she was the only one who packed a lunch for her child. Two fish sandwiches, 15–20,000 people.

In our house, we call it "God math." God math is when God's provision doesn't make sense. God math in our home was when, due to corporate restructuring, my husband and I went from two good incomes to half an income…for a full year. But God provided. It didn't make sense on paper, but it happened. We had two boys in college and were able to pay their tuition and pay our bills, and we only took $1,000 out of savings that entire year. God math.

Jesus worked God math that day with the hungry crowd. In God's economy, the miracle of multiplication happens. Jesus multiplied the two fish sandwiches and fed the crowd with baskets left over.

The third step when dealing with an obstacle or an opportunity is to remain faithful and pray. The young boy was faithful to give what he had. My husband and I were faithful to pray, work in a way that honored Him, and continue to tithe in faith. God used it, He blessed it, and He multiplied it. God math.

> Jesus got them all to sit down in groups of 50 or a hundred—they looked like a patchwork quilt of wildflowers spread out on the green grass! He took five loaves and two fish, lifted his face to heaven in prayer, blessed, broke and gave the bread to the disciples. And the disciples in turn gave it to the people. He did the same with the fish. They all ate their fill. The disciples gathered twelve baskets of leftovers. More than five thousand were at the supper.
>
> Mark 6:39–44 (MSG)

The NIV says,

> They all ate and were satisfied.
>
> Mark 6:42 (NIV)

Can you imagine how long it took the disciples to feed 15–20,000 people sitting in groups of 50–100? This was not a Chick-fil-A drive-through! This was a passing-the-basket sort of deal! I would love to see a replay of the fish sandwich feast on that day! We are told that there was more than enough.

With Jesus, there is more than enough. With Jesus, I am more than enough. Me plus Jesus equals a majority…no matter what the Enemy tries to tell me. If I get away with Jesus and rest (be still), take stock of the situation and my available resources, seek His face (pray), and be faithful… He will be faithful.

We are *imago Dei*…that makes us more than enough. It's a promise in His Word:

> No, in all these things we are more than

conquerors through him who loved us.

Romans 8:37 (NIV)

Take *that*, Satan!

CHAPTER 17

The Brady Bunch Goes to the Grand Canyon

> And do not be conformed to this world, but be transformed by the renewing of your mind, that you may prove what is that good and acceptable and perfect will of God.
>
> Romans 12:2 (NKJV)

Remember when the Brady Bunch went to the Grand Canyon (circa 1971)? (All you millennials can catch it on Nick at Nite or MeTV.) They all piled into their station wagon, pulling a trailer. It never dawned on me at the time that nine of them were in the station wagon. Nine! (Mike, Carol, Alice, Greg, Marsha, Peter, Jan, Bobby, and Cindy!) When I was about ten years old, my family and I piled into our Vista Cruiser station wagon and headed to the Grand Canyon. Our station wagon was way too small for us, and I only had one brother. We picked at each other the entire way until Dad had had enough. I can't even imagine how uncomfortable it must have been for the Brady Bunch! (Did they even have air conditioning?)

Back to the story: the Brady Bunch spent several episodes at the Grand Canyon. If you have never been there, the Grand Canyon is a site to behold. I remember racing my brother and dad up to the lookout point at the rim of the Grand Canyon. My mother crawled her way to the rail because she was afraid of heights. She had a death grip on that rail and yelled at us to stop monkeying around. My dad's words were classic, "Yep, that's a big hole, all right!" He was a sarcastic fellow, but he was fascinated by the beauty of the Grand Canyon, as was evidenced in his home movies (which made us car sick when we watched them) and slide show travelogues.

I did a little research on the birth of the Grand Canyon. There are several theories out there. The one that made the most sense to me was the "drip theory." That is where a drip becomes a creek, and a creek becomes a river. The water is constantly flowing and carving a path in the rocks and ground. Water is a powerful source of energy. It has been said that a river is capable of cutting through a large rock, not necessarily because of its power (although water is powerful), but because of its persistence.

Do you have a constant drip in your life? I have had a constant drip in my life for most of it. That drip is Satan the Accuser telling me lies about myself. One thing about Satan is that he is persistent (drip drip). He knows that if he keeps telling you lies, eventually, you will believe him (drip drip). That's when he has you…when you believe what he says about you over what God says about you (drip drip).

Satan is not just a constant drip in our lives; he was a constant drip in Jesus's life, as well. We know from the Scripture that we are not tempted (and lied to) in any way that Jesus was not also tempted…and He came out victorious. Let's visit a scene of Satan's persistence in the Gospel of Luke:

> Jesus, full of the Holy Spirit, left the Jordan and

> was led by the Spirit into the wilderness, where for forty days he was tempted by the devil. He ate nothing during those days, and at the end of them he was hungry.
>
> The devil said to him, "If you are the Son of God, tell this stone to become bread."
>
> Jesus answered, "It is written: 'Man shall not live on bread alone.'"
>
> The devil led him up to a high place and showed him in an instant all the kingdoms of the world. And he said to him, "I will give you all their authority and splendor; it has been given to me, and I give it to anyone I want to. If you worship me, it will all be yours."
>
> Jesus answered, "It is written: 'Worship the Lord your God and serve him only.'"
>
> The devil led him to Jerusalem and had him stand on the highest point of the temple. "If you are the Son of God," he said, "throw yourself down from here. For it is written:
>
> "'He will command his angels concerning you to guard you carefully; they will lift you up in their hands so that you will not strike your foot against a stone.'"
>
> Jesus answered, "It is said: 'Do not put the Lord your God to the test.'" When the devil had finished all this tempting, he left him until an opportune time."
>
> Luke 4:1–13 (NIV)

Wow! As I am reading this, several things stand out to me. The first drip that I noticed is that Satan tried to get Jesus to doubt His identity. Twice, Satan said, "*If* You are the Son of God..." That kind of reminds me of the time in Genesis when the serpent (Satan) asked Eve, "Did God really say that?" Satan likes to plant seeds of doubt. The first drip that Satan uses against me (and against you) is to doubt my identity in Christ. Second Corinthians 5:17 tells me that I am a new creation in Christ, the old stuff is gone, and I have been made brand new. I am a child of God; He paid a high price for me.

The second drip I noticed is that Satan tempted Jesus with power, authority, and wealth. All Jesus had to do was bow down and worship him. That kind of seems stupid to me because Jesus *already* owned it all. It's interesting that the stuff that Satan tied to worshiping him involved monetary reward, power, and prestige! Something to consider as we are striving to do more, have more, and be recognized more, right? Drip.

The third drip is that Satan tested Jesus to throw Himself down, and the angels would be commanded to rescue Him. Girls, Satan knows the Bible as well as we do, probably better. That is a scary thought, isn't it? During this third temptation, he quoted scripture to Jesus. Satan likes to twist scripture and *take it out of context* to meet his needs. Be careful with this one, ladies! Drip.

The good news in this passage is that Jesus models for us how to handle Satan's temptations, lies, and persistence. What did Jesus do? First, Jesus was certain of His identity. He knew that He was the Son of God, and He knew what His mission was (to save the world). Satan could not deter Him from His identity or His mission. Second, Jesus quoted the scripture back to Satan. This, ladies, is why it is so important to be in the Word, meditate on the Word, and memorize the Word. It is our weapon against Satan's fiery darts!

Therefore put on the full armor of God, so that

when the day of evil comes, you may be able to stand your ground, and after you have done everything, to stand. Stand firm them, with the belt of truth buckled around your waist, with the breastplate of righteousness in place, and with your feet fitted with the readiness that comes from the gospel of peace. In addition to all this, take up the shield of faith, with which you can extinguish all the flaming arrows of the evil one. Take the helmet of salvation and the sword of the Spirit, which is the word of God.

Ephesians 6:13–17 (NIV)

My favorite Bible study on the armor of God is by Priscilla Shirer.[11] Here are a couple of my study notes about the armor of God:

The first three pieces of armor should be my uniform every day:

- *Belt of Truth*: This is our core piece of armor that all other pieces rest upon. The ability to distinguish the Enemy's lies from God's truth is essential for success in battle.

- *Breastplate of Righteousness*: God changes me at the core. I begin to look more and more like Him (right living), but it's a daily process.

- *Shoes Fitted with the Gospel of Peace*: God is my shelter, my hiding place, and my peace. I cannot weather the storms of life without His peace. A constant attitude of gratitude will foster peace in my heart.

The next three pieces of armor are my defensive weapons against an Enemy who literally hates my guts—the first two act to guard or shield. The last piece of armor is used to go on the attack.

- ☐ *Shield of Faith*: Faith is action-oriented. I exercise faith when I *believe* and *act upon* what God is telling me. Faith and fear cannot co-exist. The Enemy can shoot his darts at me, but I can deflect them with my shield because I am "more than a conqueror in Christ."
- ☐ *Helmet of Salvation*: The Enemy is after my mind. Putting on the helmet of salvation reminds me of who I am in Christ. His Word has the power to change me and protect me. I need to be in His Word to know who I am in Him!
- ☐ *Sword of the Spirit*: This is the Word of God. It is a defensive weapon against the Enemy's attacks. Remember, Jesus used the Word of God to deflect Satan's temptations and lies.

Three out of the six pieces of armor (belt of truth, helmet of salvation, and sword of the Spirit) are Scripture-based. Suffice it to say, we need to be in the Word to ward off the Enemy's attacks.

We are made in the image of God...*imago Dei*. We have been equipped to fight off the constant drip drip drip of the Enemy. We have been given all we need. Put on that armor by *getting into the Word*!

CHAPTER 18

A Trip to Fantasy Island

> You make known to me the path of life: in your presence there is fullness of joy; at your right hand are pleasures forevermore.
>
> Psalm 16:11 (ESV)

    Yes, another television show illustration from the late '70s to early '80s. Fantasy Island was a luxury resort on a remote tropical island. The premise of the show was that travelers could fly to Fantasy Island and live out their most secret dreams. They were always greeted at the landing strip by Mr. Roarke (played by Ricardo Montalban) and his trusty sidekick, Tattoo (played by Herve Villechaize). When the plane landed, Tattoo would always shout, "Da plane! Da plane!" And thus, would start the adventure of making the traveler's dreams come true. There would usually be some sort of trauma or disaster on their way to fulfilling their fantasy, but it always ended well...because it was TV!

    One of the Enemy's favorite weapons in his arsenal to "steal, kill, and destroy" is fantasy. He likes to get in our heads with the "what-ifs." *What-ifs are dangerous. What-ifs* get us fantasizing about a different (fantasy/fake) life. *What-ifs* cause us to become discontent. Discontentment most often leads to sin, as it did in my case.

IMAGO DEI

I was a thirty-year-old overwhelmed mama. I worked full time and came home and took care of two preschool kids, grocery shopped, cooked, cleaned...you get the picture. I did what mamas the world over have been doing for centuries. But I became frustrated and discontented. My husband was an outdoorsman and enjoyed hunting, fishing, and playing golf. I was tired and overwhelmed and began to think to myself a very dangerous thought, *If I am going to raise these boys as a single mother, I might as well be single*. That *what-if* thought began to manifest itself in my mind and eventually in my heart. There was much more to our story than just that *what-if*, but that was the beginning of the end.

Like many of the plots on *Fantasy Island*, the *what-if* was not all it was cracked up to be. I am sure many of you single mothers can relate. Being a single mother is hard work! My story did end well (many, many years later), but it took a lot of hard work. Jesus had to run hard after me to redeem my life and my story. He had to change my mindset. He had to change my heart. He had to teach me that He is God, and I am not.

The Bible has a lot to say about being content. There are several verses that speak to living in the present. Living for today is called the present because it is a gift from God. He already has a good plan for my future, so there is no need to try to live there. He has already redeemed me from my past, so there is no need to dwell there. He wants me to live in the moment, *this moment*, and experience the fullness of His grace.

> There is a time for everything, and a season for every activity under the heavens.
>
> Ecclesiastes 3:1 (NIV)

When times are good, be happy; when times are bad, consider this: God has made the one as well as the other. Therefore, no one can discover anything about their future.

> Ecclesiastes 7:14 (NIV)

Be very careful, then, how you live—not as unwise but as wise, making the most of every opportunity, because the days are evil.

> Ephesians 5:15–16 (NIV)

Forget the former things, do not dwell in the past.

> Isaiah 43:18 (NIV)

Therefore do not worry about tomorrow; for tomorrow will worry about itself. Each day has enough trouble of its own.

> Matthew 6:34 (NIV)

This is the day that the Lord has made; let us rejoice and be glad in it.

> Psalm 118:24 (NIV, author's italics)

Solomon has often been considered one of the wisest men in history. It is thought that he was responsible for writing three books of the Old Testament: Song of Solomon, Proverbs, and Ecclesiastes. Song of Solomon was a love song that was written when he was a young adult. Proverbs was written while he was king, and Ecclesiastes was written in retirement.

Solomon had it all. He was successful. He was revered. He was wealthy. Solomon's life embodied an endless pursuit for meaning, and he went off the rails many times. But later in life, he discovered that it was all meaningless if God was not at the center of it all. He learned that anything that is put in God's place will never satisfy. That's when he wrote Ecclesiastes. All the way through the book, Solomon talks about how stuff cannot satisfy; only God can. He encourages us to live in the season that we are in. He reminds us that the current season is a gift and time is fleeting, so we need to make the most of *today*, today.

The apostle Paul was of the same mindset. He was all about making the most of today's opportunity. As we talked about previously, Paul got off to a rough start. He was a Pharisee of Pharisees, a highly legalistic sect. He was a persecutor of Christians…until he met Jesus on the road to Damascus.

The most highlighted and marked-up book in my Bible is the book of Philippians. It was Paul's letter to the church at Philippi, penned while he was a prisoner in Rome. It is only four short chapters, but man, it packs a big punch! Paul tells us in his letter how to finish well. I am all about finishing well because my start wasn't particularly stellar.

I don't know this to be true, but I think Paul must have been an athlete because he makes so many athletic references, particularly running, to illustrate his points:

> Not that I have already obtained all this or have already been made perfect, but I press on to take hold of that for which Christ Jesus took hold of me. Brothers, I do not consider myself yet to

> have taken hold of it. But one thing I do: Forgetting what is behind and straining toward what is ahead. I press on toward the goal to win the prize for which God has called me heavenward in Christ Jesus.
>
> Philippians 3:12–14 (NIV)

Paul could not move forward to win the prize if he was stuck in the past. He had to forget his past failures in order to press on. Otherwise, he would have been rendered ineffective. I cannot make the most of today if I am still stuck in the past. It's fun to have friends on Facebook from high school and peek at what they are doing now and see their families. But sometimes, our past can hold us hostage. Either we are ashamed of our past because of mistakes we made, or we look at it through rose-colored glasses at what could have been. Either way, there is great wisdom in making peace with the past, leaving it behind, and pressing forward.

Paul finishes his letter to the Philippians by talking about the importance of being content. Reminder: Paul is writing about contentment while imprisoned!

> I know what it is to be in need, and I know what it is to have plenty. I have learned in any and every situation, whether well fed or hungry, whether living in plenty or in want. I can do all this through him who gives me strength.
>
> Philippians 4:12–13 (NIV)

Paul had figured out that the key to being content was to live in the present, even in prison. He let go of his past, and he did not fantasize about the future. He lived in the moment and was grateful for all things. (An attitude of gratitude goes a long way in attaining contentment.) He knew that he could remain in a state of contentment because He knew *who* his source of contentment was: Jesus Christ.

Let's revisit the verse cited at the beginning of this chapter:

> You make known to me the path of life: in your presence there is fullness of joy; at your right hand are pleasures forevermore.
>
> Psalm 16:11 (ESV)

A good definition of contentment can be the fullness of joy. This verse reminds us of what Paul knew: in God's presence, there is fullness of joy—contentment.

FOMO: fear of missing out. It's an affliction that Satan loves to put on us. Satan doesn't want us to be content; he wants us to stay stuck in the past or fantasize about the future. He doesn't want us to live in the present, where contentment lies. But I have good news: we are *imago Dei*…made in the image of God. Because of this, we can leave the past behind, live a life of contentment (fully in the present), and press on to finish well.

Chapter 19

Judge Judy

> Do not judge, or you too will be judged. For in the same way you judge others, you will be judged, and with the measure you use, it will be measured to you.
>
> Matthew 7:1–2 (NIV)

If the Holy Spirit has an audible voice, I think I heard it a couple of days ago. I was in Walmart (of course), and it was a strange people day. It seemed like on every aisle I cruised down, there would be an "interesting looking" guy or gal. Did you know that there is actually a website where people have posted pictures of Walmart shoppers wearing outlandish outfits or looking "interesting"? (Man, I hope nobody has posted my picture on that website!) My internal narrative was not good. I *hope* that my internal dialogue was not reflected on my face, but I know it probably was. I was trying to be cool, but I doubt that is the sentiment that I portrayed. My momma used to tell me quite often to "fix my face." (If you know me, you know that you can probably tell what I think about something by my facial expression…it's a good thing I don't play poker because I would lose.)

Anyway, as I was shopping and "observing" my fellow

shoppers, I heard the words, "Judge Judy!" I probably just heard the words in my heart, but it sure felt like an audible proclamation to me. The sad thing is that I knew exactly what those words meant...I was judging others by their appearance. Ugh! The *one thing* that I *hate* to have done to me, I was doing to others! I was so mad at myself. I was looking at (and judging) others through the world's eyes and not through God's eyes! I was Judge Judy!

Every once in a great while, when I am flipping through the TV channels, I land on *Judge Judy* for a minute or two to see what she is up to. Judge Judy Sheindlin is a former family court judge. On her TV show, she is a no-monkey business, get-to-the-point, sarcastic kind of judge. She abhors dishonesty, and she likes to get to the bottom line in a swift manner. Her sarcasm and brutal honesty made her famous. When the Holy Spirit called me Judge Judy, I don't think He was saluting me for my discernment or quick wit. He was letting me know that I was being judgmental and, dare say, cruel.

As soon as I reflected on doing to others what I hate having done to me (being judged by appearance), these words from the apostle Paul came to mind:

> I do not understand what I do. For what I want
> to do I do not do, but what I hate I do.
>
> Romans 7:15 (NIV)

I get it, Paul. The very thing I have struggled with the most, letting others (and Satan) define me, is what I am doing to others. Here is what I am thinking about that: the things that we are the most critical of in others are the same things that we struggle with ourselves. This is where the sin of comparison creeps in. Say, for example, we are judging others by their appearance. When we do that, we compare their appearance to our own. Since I have struggled with weight all my life (or thought I did), I will use that as an example. If I see some sweet lady bulging out of her britches, I might take a quick cruise past the mirror to see if I am bulging out, as well. Basically, I am *comparing how I stack up*! That is being critical, judgmental, and unkind.

God sets boundaries in our lives because He is kind, full of compassion, and wants the best for us. His Word has a great deal to say about the sin of comparison. Here are a couple of verses to ponder:

> Not that we dare to classify or compare ourselves with some of those who are commending themselves. But when they measure themselves by one another and compare themselves with one another, they are without understanding.
>
> 2 Corinthians 10:12 (ESV)

> For am I now seeking the approval of man, or of God? Or am I trying to please man? If I were still trying to please man, I would not be a servant of God.
>
> Galatians 1:10 (ESV)

And finally, the *pièce de résistance*:

> Don't be selfish; don't try to impress others. Be humble, thinking of others as better than yourselves. Don't look out only for your own interests, but take an interest in others, too.
>
> Philippians 2:3–4 (NLT)

If I value others above myself, I am not going to make comparative judgments. Instead, I am going to have a heart of gratitude for the uniqueness that every person brings to the table. Look at who Jesus hung around with: sinners and tax collectors! (Isn't it kind of funny that the IRS agents of biblical times were considered the lowest of the low? I had to chuckle at that!)

How we see ourselves affects how we perceive others. If we see ourselves as worthy, kind, loving, and beautiful daughters of the King...we will see others through that same lens. If we see ourselves as unworthy, ugly, fat, and unlovable...we will see others through that cloudy, inaccurate lens.

I went to Israel five years ago. I am totally excited about going back to Israel this summer. It is truly a life-changing, faith-building, fall-in-love with Jesus all over again experience! When I was there, I learned about an interesting little case that was nailed to the upper right-hand side of a door casing. It is called a *Mezuzah*. (*Mezuzah* literally means doorpost in Hebrew.) The *Mezuzah* is a symbol that a Jewish family resides in that home. It also serves as a reminder to the family that inhabits the home that they have a covenant with God. Inside the *Mezuzah* is a parchment that is inscribed with the *Shema*, which is found in Deuteronomy 6:4–9:

> Hear, O Israel: The Lord our God, the Lord is one. Love the Lord your God with all your heart and with all your soul and with all your strength. These commandments that I give you today are to be on your hearts. Impress them on your children. Talk about them when you sit at home and when you walk along the road, when you lie down and when you get up. Tie them as symbols on your hands and bind them on your foreheads.

Write them on the doorframes of your houses
and your gates.

Deuteronomy 6:4–9 (NIV)

The *Shema* is a reminder to love God with all your being. I think it's interesting to note that Jesus took the *Shema* a step further. The Pharisees were trying to trick Him and asked Him which commandment was the most important. His response was stellar:

> Jesus replied, "Love the Lord your God with all your heart and with all your soul and with all your mind." This is the first and greatest commandment. And the second is like it: "Love your neighbor as yourself."

Matthew 22:37–39 (NIV)

In this encounter, Jesus added two things to the *Shema*. First, when talking about loving God, He said that in addition to loving God with all our hearts and souls, we should also love Him with all our minds. Jesus knew the battle for our hearts and souls always begins in the mind. Remember when Satan tempted Him in the desert? He repeatedly defeated temptation with the Word of God that was safely tucked away in His mind. Then, Jesus told the Pharisees that the second most important commandment was to love our neighbor as ourselves.

Judge Judy here! I did not love my fellow Walmart shopping neighbors as myself. Like I said before, I hate it when people judge me by my appearance. Yet, I was doing it right there in Walmart (and I got busted for it quickly!).

We are *all imago Dei*. We are *all* uniquely made…on purpose. If I don't see myself as created in His image and truly adored by my Creator, I'm not going to see the rest of His creation in that light either. I am a work in progress (and thank God I am!). I am so glad that He promises to finish the work that He has started in me...no more Judge Judy.

Chapter 20

Masterpiece

> See, I am doing a new thing! Now it springs up;
> do you not perceive it? I am making a way in the
> wilderness and streams in the wasteland.
>
> Isaiah 43:19 (NIV)

I live in the northwest corner of Arkansas. It is a beautiful area in the foothills of the Ozark Mountains that borders Oklahoma and Missouri. Nestled deep in the woods in the center of Bentonville is the Crystal Bridges Museum of American Art. This unique oasis in the desert museum began as a gift from Alice Walton and the Walton family (of Walmart fame). From the Crystal Bridges website: "Alice gifted her art collection to form the basis of the Crystal Bridges collection, and the Walton family gifted 120 acres of land in downtown Bentonville Arkansas as the site for the museum."[12] The museum displays American art from artists such as Norman Rockwell to Andy Warhol and everything in between. It really is truly amazing, and people travel not only from all over the United States but literally all over the world to view the collection.

My daddy was a gifted painter. He didn't start painting until he was in his forties. He loved to reproduce Thomas Kinkade's paintings with acrylic on canvas. I didn't get the painting gene, although I have tried. But I did inherit an eye for beauty and an admiration for artistry. My favorite painter is probably Claude Monet. (I don't think Crystal Bridges currently has a Monet on display; plus, he was a French painter.) I like Monet's simple, peaceful field of flowers type paintings. They are very simplistic but rich in color. "The Artist's Garden at Giverny" (1900) and "Water Lilies" (there are several) are my favorites. They are rich in color but also send out a peaceful vibe. I enjoy Crystal Bridges because I enjoy looking at wonderful masterpieces of art.

Our Creator Redeemer enjoys looking at His wonderful masterpieces of art as well. How do I know this? Because He says so in the Bible! Did you know that He calls us His masterpiece?

> God saved you by his grace when you believed. And you can't take credit for this; it is a gift from God. Salvation is not a reward for the good things we have done, so none of us can boast about it. For we are God's *masterpiece*. He has created us a new in Christ Jesus, so we can do the good things he planned for us long ago.
>
> Ephesians 2:8–10 (NLT, author's italics)

Wow! I've never thought of myself as a *masterpiece* before. (That is not exactly my thought when I look in the mirror!) What about you?

Satan does not want us to know that we are a masterpiece. He likes to use words like "mess" to define us. I heard on a podcast the other day something that went like this: "He that did not design you cannot define you!" If I had not been driving, I would have jumped up with a shout at that statement! Satan cannot define us because he did not design us. Our Creator Redeemer is the only one who can define us. I wish I had believed this bit of wisdom when I was younger…it might have changed the course of my life, and I would have avoided some heartache.

He created us. He chose us. He set us apart. We are His masterpiece. For what purpose? Look at the verse again, "So we can do the good things that He has planned for us long ago." He had a plan for us before He even created us. If we believe in Jesus and accept His gift, we are a new creation…created to do good work.

> Therefore, if anyone is in Christ, he is a new creation; old things have passed away; behold, all things have become new.
>
> 2 Corinthians 5:17 (NKJV)

"New" is a good word. Who doesn't like new? New clothes. New haircut. New car. We admire new things. Don't you know that He, our Creator Redeemer, admires us when we are new as well? Oh, He has always loved us. But when we are a new creation, our relationship with Him is enhanced. It's special.

I told you before that I love stories when the underdog wins. I also love stories of new beginnings. The story of Ruth is both. Ruth was an underdog in that she was a widow at a young age, and she was a Moabite—both characteristics were looked down upon in Bethlehem. Naomi, her mother-in-law, was a widow as well. She told Ruth to go back to her people and let them take care of her, perhaps marry again. But Ruth was loyal to Naomi:

> But Ruth replied, "Don't urge me to leave you or to turn back from you. Where you go I will go, and where you stay I will stay. Your people will

> be my people and your God my God. Where you die I will die, and there I will be buried. May the Lord deal with me, be it ever so severely, if even death separates you and me." When Naomi realized that Ruth was determined to go with her, she stopped urging her.
>
> Ruth 1:16–18 (NIV)

Time out: I've got to say this! Don't you just love the Bible? There is a story for absolutely everything that we deal with. God's Word, written well over 2,000 years ago, is so very timeless. In fact, it's still the number-one bestseller of all time!

Back to Ruth. Ruth, despite her tragedy, displays unbelievable loyalty to Naomi. (Incidentally, Naomi now wants to be called "Mara," meaning bitter, because her life isn't so great now either.) I bet she was a real joy to travel with…hashtag: Debbie Downer.

Another attractive quality of Ruth was that she was a hard worker. Instead of waiting for others to give her a handout, she went right to work. She began to glean in the fields for grain. In biblical times, gleaning was sort of a welfare system. Workers in the field would leave the corners a bit unharvested so that the poor could come behind them and collect the unharvested grain or whatever crop that was in that field. As it turned out, Ruth was gathering grain in a field that belonged to a man named Boaz. (Favor.)

Boaz was a godly man. When he checked the fields, he shouted out a blessing to those who were working for him. Ruth caught his eye, and he inquired as to who she was. The overseer basically told Boaz that she was a widow and the daughter-in-law of Naomi and that she was taking care of Naomi. And, oh, by the way…she was a really hard worker! Boaz instructed his men to leave a little extra behind for Ruth and not to touch her. They were to share their water with her when she became thirsty. (Favor.)

When Ruth went back to Naomi and shared her food and the day's wages with her, Naomi asked where she had worked.

> Then Ruth told her mother-in-law about the one at whose place she had been working. "The name of the man I worked with today is Boaz," she said.
>
> "The Lord bless him!" Naomi said to her daughter-in-law. "He has not stopped showing his kindness to the living and the dead." She added, "That man is our close relative, he is one of our guardian-redeemers."

Ruth 2:19–20 (NIV)

(Favor.)

There are no coincidences with God...it's all part of His plan. You may have heard the term "kinsman-redeemer"? A guardian-redeemer is the same thing. A kinsman-redeemer, by law, had the responsibility to act on behalf of a close relative who was in trouble or in need. In this situation, a kinsman-redeemer had the responsibility (and privilege) of restoring the widow to a place of honor in society. Isn't it just like God to provide a way when there seems to be no way? Sit in that thought for just a few seconds before we continue with our love story.

> One day Ruth's mother-in-law Naomi said to her, "My daughter, I must find a home for you, where you will be well provided for. Now Boaz, with whose women you have worked, is

> a relative of ours. Tonight he will be winnowing barley on the threshing floor. Wash, put on perfume, and get dressed in your best clothes. Then go down to the threshing floor, but don't let him know you are there until he has finished eating and drinking. When he lies down, note the place where he is lying. Then go and uncover his feet and lie down. He will tell you what to do."
>
> Ruth 3:1–4 (NIV)

The plot thickens! Isn't this great? Plotting and scheming with our home girls started way back in biblical times! Personal sidebar: when I was interested in my husband, my mom helped me "stalk" him at basketball games, track meets, and church. We thought we were sly. Turns out, he knew he was being stalked the whole time. He will laugh when he reads this because we were terrible! (Although it ended well. We've been married for over twenty-two years!) My precious grandmother even got in on the stalking business!

Boaz wakes up in the middle of the night and notices someone lying at his feet. He asks who it is, and Ruth tells him that it is she and that he is her kinsman-redeemer. He blessed her for coming to him rather than some young fella. (Favor.)

Be sure to go back and read the full story of Ruth; it's only four short chapters. After a little bit of wheeling and dealing, Ruth becomes Boaz's wife. He takes care of her, and her place in society is restored. This is better than a Hallmark movie! But it even gets better! Boaz and Ruth had a son:

> Then Naomi took the child in her arms and cared for him. The women living there said, "Naomi

has a son!" And they named him Obed. He was
the father of Jesse, the father of David.

Ruth 4:16–17 (NIV)

Ruth had a son. Ruth had a built-in babysitter in Naomi. That son is in the lineage of David. Which means that the son is in the lineage of Jesus. (Favor.)

> This is the genealogy of Jesus the Messiah the
> son of David, the son of Abraham.

Matthew 1:1 (NIV)

> Salmon the father of Boaz, whose mother was
> Ruth, Obed the father of Jesse.

Matthew 1:5 (NIV)

Ruth had a new life, a new lease on life, really. Her kinsman-redeemer rescued her, redeemed her, and restored her. Jesus Christ is our Kinsman-Redeemer. We are His masterpiece. We were created in His image, *imago Dei*. He saved us, redeemed us, and set us apart to do good things for His glory! (Favor.)

Chapter 21

Two Little Words

> You've kept track of my every toss and turn
> through the sleepless nights, each tear entered in
> your ledger, each ache written in your book.
>
> Psalm 56:8 (MSG)

I am over the moon excited to be going to Israel again this summer. My husband and I went in 2018. It was life-changing. It made the Bible come alive for us. We learned so much from Pilar, our tour guide. She was fantastic. She was a Messianic Jew from Spain. She was part historian, part culturalist, and part theologian. So much information came at us so fast that we knew we needed to go back to tie those pieces together. Reading the Bible is one thing, but when you hear the words in the place they were spoken, that's a whole other thing!

One of the things that we learned about and saw in stores in Jerusalem were little bitty glass bottles called lachrymatories. *Lacrima* is the Latin word for "tear," so a lachrymatory is a holder of tears. They are tiny bottles, usually made of glass. We heard a story about how wives would collect their tears in a bottle when their husbands went off to war so they could present them with a visual representation of their sorrow in their warrior's absence.

(Question: Was evaporation not a thing then?) That was not the only use for a lachrymatory. Mourners would also collect their tears in a bottle and bury it in the tomb with their loved ones.

Psalm 56 was written by David when he was captured by the Philistines. David talks about getting beat up daily, yet he still praises God. He remarked that "mere mortals" could do nothing to him because his trust was in God. He knew that his Father heard his prayers and was empathetic to his pain. This verse illustrates that God felt David's pain:

> You keep track of all my sorrows. You have collected all my tears in your bottle. You have recorded each one in your book.
>
> Psalm 56:8 (NLT)

Jesus always meets us at our point of need and sits with us in it. He created us for a relationship with Him, and He truly enters our pain…if we let Him. Another example in the Bible of how He enters our pain (and collects our tears) comes from the shortest verse in the Bible. Just two little words that pack a whole lot of punch:

> Jesus wept.
>
> John 11:35 (NIV)

This is an interesting story. At the beginning of John Chapter 11, we learn that Jesus greatly loved Martha, her sister Mary, and their brother, Lazarus. How special that John calls out Jesus's love for the trio. But how odd what John says next:

> Now Jesus loved Martha and her sister and Lazarus. So when he heard that Lazarus was sick, he stayed where he was two more days.
>
> John 11:5–6 (NIV)

I find it interesting that Jesus lingered and did not go straight away to heal Lazarus. I guess if you are the Creator and Savior of the world, you don't need to get in a hurry because you know that you have the power to raise the dead. Or was there another reason that Jesus lingered?

> So then he told them plainly, "Lazarus is dead and for your sake I am glad I was not there, *so that you may believe*. But let us go to him."
>
> John 11:14–15 (NIV, author's italics)

There's the reason. Had He gone while Lazarus was just sick, the disciples would have seen Him heal Lazarus. But waiting until after he was good and dead (four days)…now *that* was a huge miracle. They would be able to witness Jesus's ultimate power, to raise the dead to new life. Perhaps this was Him foreshadowing His own death, burial, and resurrection. Jesus was showing the disciples (and others) that He had the power to conquer the grave.

Let's look into what happens next:

> When Martha heard that Jesus was coming she went out to meet him, but Mary stayed home.
>
> John 11:20 (NIV)

Remember the story of Mary and Martha? Mary is

the one who sat at the feet of Jesus and just soaked Him in. Martha, on the other hand, was the doer. She was busy scurrying around in her hostess duties and eventually complained to Jesus about her lazy sister. Jesus reminded Martha that Mary had chosen the better thing…to dwell. In this story, busybody Martha runs out to meet Jesus. But this time, she expressed her faith over her frustration (after a bit of her signature whining):

> "Lord," Martha said to Jesus, "if you had been here my brother would not have died. But I know that even now God will give you whatever you ask."
>
> John 11:21–22 (NIV)

Jesus responded in what had become a teachable moment for all present.

> Jesus said to her, "Your brother will rise again."
>
> Martha answered, "I know he will rise again in the resurrection at the last day."
>
> Jesus said to her, "I am the resurrection and the life. The one who believes in me will live, even though they die; and whoever lives by believing in me will never die. Do you believe this?"
>
> "Yes, Lord," she replied, "I believe that you are the Messiah, the Son of God, who is to come into the world."
>
> John 11:23–27 (NIV)

After Martha's conversation with Jesus, she went to tell Mary where Jesus was. Mary ran to meet Jesus. When she saw Him, she fell at His feet and basically said the same thing Martha did about Jesus being too late. When Jesus saw her and the Jews that came with her weeping, the scripture said that He was deeply moved. He entered into their pain (even knowing that He was going to bring Lazarus back to life). He was hurting because they were hurting. Here it is, the shortest verse in the Bible:

> Jesus wept.
>
> John 11:35 (NIV)

In our suffering, we need the truth that is found in verse 25: He is the resurrection and the life. We need to believe in Him. In our suffering, we also need to remember that He enters into our pain (verse 35). Jesus wept. He weeps with me. He weeps with you. If this lachrymatory is a thing in heaven, can you imagine how big His would have to be? Truthfully, the verse about Him collecting our tears in a bottle is just an illustration of His deep love for us and how He enters into our pain.

Back to the story. I love what Jesus tells them all before Lazarus comes back from death:

> Then Jesus said, "Did I not tell you that if you believe you will see the glory of God?"
>
> John 11:40 (NIV)

You know how the story of Lazarus ends. Lazarus was bad dead in the grave for four days. By then, he was pretty stinky. Jesus tells Lazarus to come out and tells onlookers to take the grave clothes off him. (I bet they did it in a flash because of the smell.) Or maybe...they didn't. Maybe all they could smell and experience was the glory of God.

Back to verse 40. If I believe…if you believe…we will see the glory of God. He came to give us an abundant life. He didn't come to give us a mediocre life. He went to all the trouble to create us in His image (*imago Dei*); why wouldn't He give us an abundant life? If we believe in Him, we will see the glory of God!

Chapter 22

Lost Luggage

> Your beauty should not come from outward adornment, such as elaborate hairstyles and wearing of gold jewelry or fine clothes. Rather, it should be that of your inner self, the unfolding beauty of a gentle and quiet spirit, which is of great worth in God's sight.
>
> 1 Peter 3:3–4 (NIV)

Remember me telling you earlier that I could hardly wait for our repeat trip to Israel? Well, my husband and I just got back from a ten-day trip with a group from our church. My prayer in the days and weeks leading up to the trip was that God would teach me what He wanted me to know about Him while in His country. I also asked Him to give me a verse for the trip. He gave me a verse that is found in Jeremiah 29. We are all familiar with verse 11, but have you really looked past that verse? I believe that verse 13 is probably the condition for His fulfilling His good plan in our lives that He revealed in verse 11:

> When you seek me you will find me, when you seek me with all of your heart.
>
> Jeremiah 29:13 (NIV)

The flight from Arkansas to Tel Aviv was a three-hopper. A lot can go wrong (luggage-wise) when you have to make that many connections. We were a group of ninety-plus sojourners, and four did not arrive in Tel Aviv with their luggage. I guess that is really pretty good odds unless you are one of the four who arrived with no luggage. That would be me.

To say that I have the gift of administration is an understatement. I have lists for my lists, complete with table of contents. It's a slight exaggeration, but you get the picture. I carefully planned, purchased, and packed my outfits for the trip, complete with contingencies. One contingency that I was not prepared for was not receiving my luggage when we reached Tel Aviv. Luckily, I packed a carry-on with two outfits, jammies, makeup, and a toothbrush, which came in mighty handy.

The first two days were no big deal because I had my two outfits. Day three was a bit scary because we were changing hotels and moving on to Jerusalem from Tiberias. I ran out of clean clothes, so I began to buy T-shirts to wear and washed my pants in the sink to wear again. I became frantic that last night in Tiberias when my luggage did not arrive and began to cry. Steve, my husband, reminded me why we were there and to not let Satan distract me from what Jesus was trying to do in me.

That night was a fitful night of sleep. I woke up at two o'clock and stayed awake until four. So many things were going through my head as I began to pray. The first thing that came into my head was the verse about the lilies of the field. (Ladies, I cannot stress enough how important it is to get into the Word. So many times in my life, verses have popped into my head that were relevant to a current situation that I was dealing with. His Word is true. His Word is relevant. And His Word never returns void.)

> "Therefore I tell you, do not worry about your life, what you will eat or drink; or about your body, *what you will wear*. Is not life more than food, and the body more than clothes? Look at the birds of the air; they do not sow or reap or store away in barns, and yet your heavenly Father feeds them. Are you not much more valuable than they? Can any one of you by worrying add a single hour to your life?
>
> And why do you *worry about clothes*? See how the flowers of the field grow. They do not labor or spin. Yet Solomon in all his splendor was dressed like one of these. If that is how God clothes the grass of the field, which is here today and tomorrow is thrown into the fire, will he not much more clothe you—you of little faith?"
>
> Matthew 6:25–30 (NIV, author's italics)

How relevant is that? The next thing that popped into my mind was the Michael W. Smith version of the song "The Heart of Worship."[13] It began to play on repeat in my head. The song is all about stripping everything away and coming empty-handed to the Father, offering only my worship. At that moment, I knew I needed to give Him my stripped away, arms raised, hands open, and fully present worship. That is what He required of me, and that is what I did. For the next several mornings, Steve and I worshiped to that song as we prepared our hearts for the day.

The third thing that popped into my head was the words, "I am enough." Wow! He is enough. Period. Remember what I said had been my prayer for weeks leading up to the Israel trip? I prayed that He would teach me what He wanted me to know about Him. That was it. He wanted me to know that He is enough!

The Enemy's goal was to distract me from what Jesus wanted to do in my heart. Satan would have us believe that we must dress a certain way or look a certain way to fit in or belong. I'll admit I have always wanted to dress like everybody else. But God showed me clearly in the early morning hours that my clothes did not matter. Whether or not my luggage caught up with me did not matter. The only thing that mattered was my getting back to the heart of worship and believing that *He is enough*.

Bad hair days don't matter. Bad clothes days don't matter. Having all the "things" doesn't matter. We are *imago Dei*, created in His very own image. That matters.

By the way, my luggage caught up to me at 10:30 p.m. on day four in Jerusalem. I had clean clothes (and so many choices) to begin day five with!

Chapter 23

Jesus and Naps

> Six days do your work, but on the seventh day do not work; so that your ox and your donkey may rest, and so that the slave born in your household and the foreigner living among you may be refreshed.
>
> Exodus 23:12 (NIV)

We were born into a performance-based society. At my previous company, I had the opportunity to take a couple of jobs at the home office. I never wanted to go in-house for a couple of reasons. One reason was obvious: I did not want to move away from my family. The other reason was a little more covert. At the home office, there was great pressure (and pride) in being the first to arrive for work and the last to leave. A ten to twelve-hour workday was not uncommon, and I wanted no part of that. My priorities have always been faith, family, and then work, and I have never been shy about expressing it. When we get our priorities out of order, things begin to go wonky.

> But seek first his kingdom and his righteousness, and all these things will be given to you as well.
>
> Matthew 6:33 (NIV)

The Enemy (and society) likes to tell us that the busier we are, the better. Satan knows if he can keep us busy, he can wear us down. Busyness separates you from others, and it separates you from God. Busyness is an isolation strategy, and that's where Satan does his best work.

From the beginning of creation, our Creator Redeemer wanted us to stop striving and performing and rest in His presence. So much so that He modeled rest for us:

> By the seventh day God had finished the work he had been doing, so on the seventh day he rested from all his work. Then God blessed the seventh day and made it holy, because on it he rested from all the work of creating that he had done.
>
> Genesis 2:2–3 (NIV)

Two things are important to glean from this passage. The first thing is that God ordains work! It's good to work. Working with excellence and integrity is an act of worship. Colossians 3:23–24 tells us that we should work as if working for the Lord. In other places in the Bible, God warns us about not working. He goes as far as to say if you don't work, then you should not eat! Laziness was definitely not listed as a spiritual gift.

The second important thing that we need to get out of this passage is the importance of rest. I've said it before: if God repeats Himself in the Bible, we need to pay attention. He repeats Himself for extra emphasis. He repeats Himself because it is important. In two short sentences, God models for us the importance of rest. He rested from the work (also repeated) that He had been doing. Did He rest because He was tired? Absolutely not; He is our omnipotent God! He rested to model for us the importance of rest. Why was rest so important to God? Because He knew that a tired body, mind, and soul was an opportunity for Satan to throw a party. Not only did God create the world, but He also created work, and He created rest. Essentially, He created balance. When our lives get out of balance (priorities), chaos ensues.

For about five years, I was a regional account manager covering five states. For the most part, I flew out on Mondays and flew home on Thursdays. Steve, my sweet husband, knew that I would hit the wall both physically and mentally on Thursday nights at about eight o'clock. He would always tell me to go soak in a bath and go watch TV in bed and rest. He knew my limitations; I knew my limitations. I was *done* by Thursday and not good for much. Guess who else is aware of our limitations? Check this verse out:

> For He knows our frame.
>
> Psalm 103:14a (NKJV)

A couple of weeks ago, I was encouraged to apply for a newly created federal account team. I had a phone interview and didn't hear back for a couple of weeks, so I figured that it was a done deal. While in Israel, I received two invitations via e-mail for two panel interviews. The day after I got back from Israel, I had both interviews (a bit jet-lagged, I might add.) I prayed before each interview that if the new position was not God's best for me, He would shut that door.

Conversely, I prayed if that was where He wanted me to be, He would need to move mountains to make it possible. The job was a great promotion, but it came at a cost. I would be flying every week again. Was I up for it? Was this what I really needed to be doing with a mom nearing the end of her journey? I had a lot of questions, but I was resolved to be content wherever God placed me. Yesterday, I got a call from the executive director of that division. I did not get the job. I was not disappointed for even a smidge of a minute. I did not want to be where God did not call me to be. When you step outside of your calling, it becomes a struggle. He knew my frame. His answer was "no" or "not now," and that's okay.

He created us. He knows what we are made of. He knows what we are capable of. And He knows what our limitations are. That's why He ordained rest. Rest is a God-given gift.

My worth is not connected to my work. Your worth is not connected to your work. Sit in that for a moment. That's a tough one for a Type-A personality like me to believe. I am that proverbial hamster in the hamster wheel, always running, always striving, but getting nowhere. (Unless you consider exhaustion as somewhere.) Because historically, I have not believed that I am *imago Dei* (created in His image), I have always strived to work harder and smarter than my colleagues. He wants us to stop striving and rest in Him:

> He says, "Be still and know that I am God; I will be exalted among the nations, I will be exalted in the earth."
>
> Psalm 46:10 (NIV)

That has always been a hard verse for me. Being still is not something that I do naturally. I have to be intentional about being still. Perhaps you suffer from the same affliction. Stillness is an active, not a passive pursuit. I did Ann Voskamp's *Waymaker*[14] Bible study last year. In it, she talks about the fact that a heart that is still can see God. What a great word! I can't get to know Him if I am not still enough to see Him, to hear His voice, and to abide with Him. He wants me to rest so that I can dwell. I can only be still when I get off that hamster wheel of performance. I once told a friend that Jesus talks to me in my dreams. Upon hearing my statement, he came back with, "He has to because that is the only time you are quiet enough to hear His voice!" Yes, I am quite verbose, and there is a lot of truth in his words!

Jesus's ministry was fast and furious. He was thirty when he started His ministry and thirty-two when He finished the work. He prepared His whole life for ministry, yet it only lasted three short years. He performed miracles everywhere He went. He caused the lame to walk and the blind to see. He taught in temples and synagogues. He was constantly pursued by crowds. Yet, He was very disciplined about getting away to pray and rest.

> But Jesus often withdrew to lonely places and prayed.
>
> Luke 5:16 (NIV)

Jesus understood the importance of getting away and resting, recharging, and abiding with His Father. Christoformity is a churchy term meaning to pattern your life after the life of Christ. It's impossible to get it right; that's where grace comes into play. But we can look at things that He did and adopt them into our own lives. He modeled the importance of rest. He also modeled the concept of vacation. After all, vacation is the act of escaping from work, right? Jesus was fully God and fully man. He needed an occasional nap. He needed an occasional vacation from work. Those are two important things that I can really get behind. Jesus and naps!

    Satan would have us believe that we must keep striving and that our worth is determined by our work. Jesus reminds us that naps (and rest) are holy. We are *imago Dei*, and rest is God ordained.

Chapter 24

Chanel Perfume

> For the Son of Man came to seek and save the lost.
>
> Luke 19:10 (NIV)

Perhaps the biggest lie the Enemy tries to tell us is that we are too dirty to come to Jesus. Poppycock! (Super biblical term.) Jesus did not come for the righteous; He came for the lost. Churches are not houses for the holy; churches are hospitals for those in need of healing (from sin).

There is such a huge difference between religion and relationship. Jesus abhorred religion. Religion is all about keeping rules and less about relationships. He created us, every one of us, for a relationship with Him. No matter how righteous. (According to Romans 3:10, there is not one single person who is righteous.) No matter how sinful. He came for *all*.

Look at the red letters in your Bible. The red letters are Jesus's words. He gives many examples of how He came for the lost, the unlovely, the unholy, and the messy. Remember the story of Zacchaeus? He was a little bitty guy who climbed up in a tree so he could lay eyes on the One called Jesus. Jesus spotted him and told him to come down because He was going to hang out with him at his house. Zacchaeus was considered a sinner and a cheater because he worked for the IRS of that day, overcharged people, and pocketed the proceeds. Of course, Jesus knew all of this about Zacchaeus, but He wanted to have dinner with him anyway. Zacchaeus was so touched that he vowed to give all the money he had extorted back four-fold. Jesus remarked that salvation (King Jesus) had come to his house today. Don't you know that the townspeople were astonished that Jesus came to hang out with and save the lowest of the low? What an example of grace for all to see.

Jesus used parables to share His heart with His people. By definition, a parable is a short story that the audience can relate to that illustrates a spiritual principle. Mark 15 is chock-full of parables about how Jesus came for the lost, the messy.

The first parable He tells is the story about the lost sheep, one of my favorites because I can relate to it. We've talked about it earlier. The shepherd left the ninety-nine sheep and passionately pursued the one that wandered off. When he finds the one that wandered off, he puts it lovingly over his shoulders and takes it home. Then he throws a party because his lost sheep was found.

The second parable Jesus tells is the one about the lost coin. Same concept. A woman has ten coins; she loses one and methodically searches for it. When she finds it, she calls her friends together to celebrate because the lost coin has been found.

Perhaps the most famous of parables in Luke 15 is the story of the lost son, a.k.a. the prodigal son. The second-born son got tired of working and wanted his father to pay him his part of the inheritance. He travels off and squanders his inheritance on play, people, and parties. He runs out of money and gets a job feeding pigs. He is so destitute that he begs for food, but nobody helps him out. He goes back to his father with the idea of begging him for a job as one of his servants. His father sees him far off in the distance and runs to meet him. He anticipated (and hoped for) his son's return and watched daily with expectation. The father threw a party at his son's return because he once was lost and now is found.

My favorite example of Jesus's desire to save the messy is the story of the alabaster jar of Chanel perfume.

> When one of the Pharisees invited Jesus to have dinner with him, he went to the Pharisee's house and reclined at the table. A woman in town who lived a sinful life learned that Jesus was eating at the Pharisee's house, so she came there with an alabaster jar of perfume. As she stood behind him at his feet weeping, she began to wet his feet with her tears. Then she wiped them with her hair, kissed them and poured perfume on them.
>
> Luke 7:36–38 (NIV)

What a beautiful act of sold-out, all-in worship! There is so much to unpack here. First, Jesus was having dinner with the Pharisees. Pharisees were considered righteous men because they kept the law. But we know from scripture that they had a head knowledge of Jesus but not a heart knowledge of Him. Yet, Jesus came to save them.

It is said that the woman led a sinful life. Many theologians speculate that she was a prostitute. It was pretty gutsy of her to push through a crowd and barge in uninvited because she wanted to be in the presence of King Jesus. Her barging in was premeditated. She had to have run home when she heard that Jesus was coming so she could grab her most treasured possession, the alabaster jar of expensive perfume. I had to look up the significance of alabaster. It was treasured because it was extremely rare and translucent and often carved into beautiful creations. It was filled with expensive perfume. If, indeed, she was a prostitute, then she was about to lay a very important "tool of the trade" at Jesus's feet. That alabaster jar was full of so much more than just an expensive perfume. It contained years' worth of her sin, sorrow, and shame. By grabbing the alabaster jar of perfume, she was signifying that she was "all in." Her intent was to leave her past behind and follow Jesus. Notice she did not get cleaned up and un-messy... she came to Jesus *just as she was* and gave Him all that she had.

Simon, the holier than thou Pharisee, had a fit about her anointing Jesus with such an expensive perfume. Check out Jesus's response:

> Then he turned toward the woman and said to Simon, "Do you see this woman? I came into your house. You did not give me any water for my feet, but she wet my feet with her tears and wiped them with her hair. You did not give me a kiss, but this woman, from the time I entered, has not stopped kissing my feet. You did not put oil on my head, but she has poured perfume on my feet. Therefore, I tell you, her many sins have been forgiven—as her great love has shown. But whoever has been forgiven little loves little."
>
> Luke 7:44–47 (NIV)

The sinful woman had the right "heartitude." She came to Jesus broken and surrendered. She did not get all cleaned up. She did not listen to the Enemy's voice trying to condemn and shame her. She came just as she was, fully surrendered.

> Then Jesus said to her, "Your sins are forgiven."
>
> The other guests began to say among themselves, "Who is this who even forgives sins?"
>
> Jesus said to the women, "Your faith has saved you; go in peace."
>
> Luke 7:48–50 (NIV)

Wow! What a Savior. He truly came to seek and save the lost. He demonstrates over and over in the Bible that we can come to Him just as we are, messiness and all. He demonstrates over and over that He relentlessly pursues us and celebrates our homecoming.

Her sin (and yours and mine) does not disqualify us from God's amazing, restorative grace. Because we are *imago Dei*, there is redeeming grace for all at the foot of the cross. He seeks and saves *all* who are lost…especially the messy.

Chapter 25

YMCA

> Jesus has the last word on everything and everyone, from angels to armies. He's standing right alongside God, and what he says goes.
>
> 1 Peter 3:22 (MSG)

Admit it. When you read the title of this chapter, the song "YMCA" by the Village People (circa 1978) started playing on repeat in your head, right? It was a big deal when I was in about the tenth grade, and it is still a fun dance song at weddings forty-five years later! YMCA (the place, not the song) was a hard lesson for me when I was about sixteen years old. You see, I have always had this "affliction" in my life. Maybe you have suffered or still suffer from the same affliction. The affliction is that I like to try to get in the final word. Often, getting the last word comes with a cost. Most of the time, that cost is high enough that it totally is not worth it.

When I was sixteen, we moved from Ft. Scott, KS, to Little Rock, AR. I was a sophomore in high school and loved my town, loved my school, and loved my friends. Moving in the middle of my sophomore year to a new, big city was traumatic. I started my new school in the middle of the year. It was hard making new friends because all my new classmates had gone to school together since grade school. I was an unwelcome guest; at least, I felt like I was. I moped around and cried for weeks. I had no place to go and no friends to run around with. The YMCA was behind our house a few blocks away. It had an indoor swimming pool, tennis courts, a weight room, and a dance studio with classes. Aerobics was a big deal around that time. (Remember Olivia Newton-John and "Physical"?) My dad got tired of my moping and suggested that we visit the YMCA to see if we wanted to join. That perked up a sixteen-year-old's heart. We went and visited. It was fabulous and nothing like anything that our former small town had to offer. We toured the facilities and looked at the list of classes. I was all in… till I wasn't. I was disrespectful to my dad. He warned me that I was walking on thin ice. That's when my affliction took over. I had to have the last word. He was done. They did not join the YMCA until I left for college. My desire to have the last word cost me yet again.

You would think that I would have outgrown the desire to get in the last word by now, wouldn't you? My husband can testify that that is definitely not the case. (Much to my chagrin.) I had a couple of things that happened at work this week where I had the last word (or thought I did). During my quiet time, just out of the blue, these words came to mind, and I wrote them in my journal, "I (God) get the final word!" Well, that was obviously the Holy Spirit, so I had to confess some things this morning and ask for forgiveness. I am reminded of what I used to say to my kids when they apologized to me, "Don't tell me you're sorry if we're going to be here again!" I wonder if that is what Jesus thought this morning when I asked for forgiveness. Hmmm.

I'm not totally sure of what He meant when He said He would have the final word. Does that have to do with my work? Does it have to do with my relationships? Does it have to do with my obedience? I am not sure, but I will be unpacking that over the next few days to weeks. What I do know is that I will be more aware when in conversation with coworkers, my spouse, and others. Perhaps a yield sign will come up in my mind, asking me if I really need to say what I am thinking. Do I really need to have the final say?

The Enemy would like us to rush into conversation without really thinking about it. The Enemy would like us to think that we need to have the final say every time. Wanting the final say is selfish and self-centered. The funny thing is, in an argument, the final word is never the final word. Even if no words are spoken, the final word circulates around in our minds. It is never final, and that leads to a lack of peace for all the participants.

This summer, our church is studying the book of Ephesians. This morning's sermon was in Ephesians 5. The very first verse made me start to think about this whole last-word scenario.

> Therefore, be imitators of God, as beloved children. And walk in love, as Christ loved us and gave himself up for us a fragrant offering and sacrifice of God.
>
> Ephesians 5:1–2 (ESV)

I like the version in The Message Version even better because it expands on Christ's love:

> Watch what God does, and then you do it, like children who learn proper behavior from their parents. Mostly what God does is love you. Keep company with him and learn a life of love.

> Observe how Christ loved us. His love was not cautious but extravagant. He didn't love in order to get something from us but to give everything of himself to us. Love like that.
>
> Ephesians 5:1–2 (MSG)

He modeled appropriate behavior for us like a daddy models appropriate behavior for his children. Why? *Because He loves us*! We teach our children how to act in this world because we love them and want them to live a happy, healthy, and peaceful life.

The word "love" is mentioned six times in just two verses. Remember what I have said a couple of times previously in this book? When God repeats Himself, we need to pay attention. It is all about love! We love because He loved us first!

When my eighty-six-year-old mom and I finish up a phone call, this is what our ending conversation sounds like:

I say, "I love you, Momma!"

She always responds with, "I love you more!"

I finish with, "You may have loved me longer, but definitely not more!"

When we think about the love of God, we can be confident of two facts: He has loved us longer, and He definitely loves us more! After all, He created us in His image (*imago Dei*)!

My big takeaway from the sermon this morning is that we are to walk in love. Maybe a better translation would be to walk *out* our love. Having the last word is not walking out my love. I am reminded of a verse in Micah that asks what God requires of us:

> He has shown you, O mortal, what is good. And what does the Lord require of you? To act justly and to love mercy and to walk humbly with your God.
>
> Micah 6:8 (NIV)

I love that verse so much that I have it engraved on a sign in my bedroom as a reminder of what God requires of me. Acting with justice and mercy and walking humbly are all ways that I can walk out my love for others. They are all ways that others can see Jesus in me. They will know that we are Christ's followers by our love. The converse is also true. If we act selfishly (insisting on having the last word), will they know we are Christians? (An ouch for me this week!)

Just as our opening verse states, Jesus will have the final say. He will have the final say in our lives. He will have the final say in America. He will have the final say in the world. He ultimately will have the final say in the universe. He is our Creator Redeemer, Elohim (Creator of all)...and that gives Him the final say (not me!).

The comforting fact about Jesus having the final say is that every Word that comes from His mouth will not return void:

> So shall my word be that goes out from my mouth; it shall not return to me empty, but it shall accomplish that which I purpose, and shall succeed in the thing for which I sent it.
>
> Isaiah 55:11 (ESV)

What is the purpose for which He sent His words out? He sent His words out to tell us that He loves us. He sent

IMAGO DEI

His words out to draw us to Him. He sent His words out to redeem us and save us. That is how He walks out His love for us.

We are *imago Dei*, created in His image. He created us to love like He loves…not to have the last word.

Chapter 26

One Big Lie

> Do nothing out of selfish ambition or vain conceit, but in humility consider others better than yourselves. Each of you should look not only to your own interests, but also to the interests of others.
>
> Philippians 2:3–4 (NIV)

For thousands and thousands of years, the Spinner of Spoof (Satan) has been telling us *one big lie*. (By the way, one of the synonyms for "spoof" is "deception.") You can watch the news and see evidence that, indeed, that lie is alive and well, especially right here in America. That lie plagues all of us.

My grandbabies are three years old. A boy and a girl. Perfect in every way (in Nonna's eyes). At the age of three, actually before the age of three, they bought into the lie. I see the lie when they are at play. I see the lie when they are eating. I hear the lie in stories from their daycare. There's no escaping it. We all bought into the lie practically from birth.

You've probably guessed what the lie is: *it's all about me*! As much as I hate to admit it, it's not all about me. More bad news…it's not all about you, either. But we live it. We see it everywhere. All the selfishness and ugliness in this world are a direct result of the lie that it is all about us.

For a long time now, I have thought that traffic accidents are a direct result of the lie. After all, people have wrecks when they want to have their own way, right? Think about it. If drivers took their time and were courteous to the other drivers around them, the chance of having a wreck would be diminished considerably.

There is such a spirit of entitlement in the world today. We oldies think that the younger generation has the market cornered on a sense of entitlement and deservedness. But the fact of the matter is, we seasoned adults have that same spirit (i.e., we get to retire because we've *earned* it!) I was talking to a twenty-something professional young lady, and she was telling me about her planned upcoming trip. The trip sounded wonderful. She does life at a hard pace, and I am sure a respite was much needed. But the last three little words she said about the trip really got to me: "I deserve it!"

No, I don't deserve retirement. That twenty-something young lady doesn't deserve a vacation. We, in fact, don't deserve anything. What we do deserve is judgment. What we do deserve is a penalty for our sins. But what we get instead is undeserved pardon…grace.

Satan tells me that it's all about me. When I grumble and complain, it's because I have a me-centered focus. If I have a spirit of entitlement, with me at the center of my universe, then "it" will never be enough. I will always want more attention. I will always want more recognition. I will always want more stuff. I will always want more… (you fill in the blank).

Mercy! Holding our place at the center of the universe would be a tough job! Can you imagine how much responsibility it would be to hold everything together? If it was all about you or me, we would be responsible for everybody else's happiness as well, not just our own. Personally, I don't know if I would want that job! All the griping and complaining? No. Thank. You.

When I was in high school, my youth group leader had us memorize a few verses from Colossians. I memorized them because it was a competition, and Lord knows I needed to excel to feel accepted! (Lie from Satan.) I memorized those words, but I did not fully understand them nor apply them to my heart. Now, I get it:

> The Son is the image of the invisible God, the firstborn over all creation. For in him all things were created: things in heaven and on earth, visible and invisible, whether thrones or powers or rulers or authorities; *all things* have been created through him and for him. He is before *all things*, and in him *all things* hold together.
>
> Colossians 1:15–17 (NIV, author's italics)

Whew! That sure takes the pressure off! Jesus is at the center of it all! In Jesus, *all things* are held together. I am not at the center of my universe or anybody else's, so I don't have to keep it all going, and I am not responsible for anybody else's happiness.

I used to be a hospital account manager in the world of HIV. The science of HIV is a deep, physiological, intracellular science. About five years ago, I was having lunch with an experienced nurse practitioner in Tupelo. Becky had been treating HIV for over twenty-seven years. There was a physiology book lying on the lunch table. As I was waiting for her to come back to lunch, I began to thumb through that physiology book. I arrived at a beautiful picture of laminin, the cell adhesion molecule of the body. Its sole purpose at the molecular level is to *hold things together*. The most miraculous thing about laminin is that it is in the shape of a cross! That's right! The molecule that holds everything together in the body is shaped like a cross! When Becky came back for lunch, I was excited to share the verses from Colossians with her and show her the picture that I found in her physiology book.

> He is before all things, and in him all things hold together.
>
> Colossians 1:17 (NIV)

I love the consistency in God's Word! Over 2,000 years ago, we were told that in Christ, all things are held together. The scientific proof still exists today. Laminin, the cell adhesion molecule in our bodies, is shaped like a cross. There are no accidents with God. He was meticulous in His creation. The evidence is clear.

He is before *all things*. In Him, *all things* are held together. He is at the center of it all. I am not. The pressure is on Him, not on me.

Paul wrote four letters to believers from a prison cell. Prison was not exactly a place where it was all about him, yet he taught us about a better way to win the battle in your mind:

> Don't fret or worry. Instead of worrying, pray. Let petitions and praises shape your worries into prayers, letting God know your concerns. Before you know it, a sense of God's wholeness, everything coming together for good, will come and settle you down. It's wonderful what happens when Christ displaces worry at the center of your life.
>
> Summing it all up, friends. I'd say you'll do best by filling your minds and meditating on things true, noble, reputable, authentic, compelling,

gracious—the best, not the worst; the beautiful
not the ugly; things to praise, not things to curse.
Put into practice what you learned from me,
what you heard and saw and realized. Do that,
and God, who makes everything work together,
will work you into his most excellent harmonies.

> Philippians 4:6–9 (MSG)

Who doesn't love harmony? When we stop being self-centered and start being Christ-centered, harmony begins to exist. Harmony is walking in step with Jesus, and it brings joy and peace instead of discouragement and discontentment.

The science of neuropathways says that anytime you try to stop a negative behavior (or thought), a vacuum is created. To be successful in eliminating that negative behavior or thought, you must replace it with a positive one. Paul tells us that the way to achieve harmony is to let go of worry and put worship in its place. Praise and panic cannot coexist. You either have one or the other. An attitude of gratitude goes a long way in replacing worry and other negative thoughts. Paul tells us that praise is the antidote for worry.

Paul goes on to tell us the things that we should fill our minds with. Notice all the things are positive: true, noble, reputable, authentic, compelling, gracious, the best, the beautiful, and things that are praiseworthy. Those aren't exactly things that the Enemy wants us to set our minds on.

The big lie is that it's all about me. Jesus's truth is that it's all about Him, which takes the pressure off us. He is our Creator Redeemer. He is our sovereign God. When we "stay in our own lane," peace and harmony are to be had. We are *imago Dei*, and He never meant for us to carry His burden.

Chapter 27

Dogs Do Fly

> Turn to me and have mercy, For I am alone and in deep distress.
>
> Psalm 25:16 (NLT)

Medals should be awarded to all the single moms out there. I was a single mom, and it is hard work, definitely not for the faint of heart. I bought into the lie that if I was going to be a single mom in my marriage, I might as well have the "perks" of being a single mom. If you are a young lady, you need to tune in to what I am about to tell you: there are no "perks" to being a single mom. It's hard. It's messy. It's lonely. Commit your marriage to God. Stay in the fight. Satan wants to destroy families, but your Creator Redeemer can bring beauty from ashes. (Of course, there are extenuating circumstances like safety issues, infidelity, and abuse.)

I was having one of my single mom moments. My boys were probably about five and eight years old. Sometimes, I would get so frustrated at dinner time, trying to be creative with their dinners when they only liked a couple of things. It was hot dog night. I, myself, am not a fan of hot dogs, but it was a safe bet for the boys. One liked his dog with ketchup only; the other one liked his fully loaded. I committed an unpardonable sin. I accidentally put mustard on the ketchup-only kid's dog. His reaction was immediate, complete with tears. He wailed, "I said I wanted ketchup only!" At that, I sailed the hot dog through the air. He ducked, and it hit the wall. Laughter spread throughout the kitchen. Hint: mustard stains wallpaper. Yes, dogs (hot dogs) do fly!

Why did I tell you the story of the flying dog? It's because, at that moment, I felt alone in the battle. In fact, I felt alone in the battle a lot. But the truth of the matter was that I was never truly alone. My parents were wonderful at stepping in and helping, and I appreciated them so much for their investment in my boys' lives. I was so in survival mode that I forgot the truth that my Jesus was right there with me, lockstep in the battle beside me.

> When you go through deep waters, I will be with you. When you go through rivers of difficulty, you will not drown. When you walk through the fire of oppression, you will not be burned up; the flames will not consume you. For I am the Lord, your God, the Holy One of Israel, your Savior.
>
> Isaiah 43:2–3 (NLT)

King Nebuchadnezzar of Babylon went to Jerusalem and seized it. He captured and brought back sacred objects to be placed in the storehouse for his god (little "g"), along with several young men to be groomed to enter his service.

> "Select only strong, healthy and good-looking young men," he said. "Make sure they are well versed in every branch of learning, and gifted with knowledge and good judgment, and are suited to serve in the royal palace. Train these

> young men in the language and literature of Babylon." The king assigned them a daily ration of food and wine from his own kitchens. They were to be trained for three years, and then they would enter his royal service.
>
> Daniel 1:4–5 (NLT)

The four Jewish young men that they selected were named Daniel, Hananiah, Mishael, and Azariah. The very first change in their lives at the hands of King Neb was a name change. In Jewish tradition, naming a child is more than just a label. A name represents a child's identity; it is almost prophetic. Jewish tradition goes as far as to say a name tells a story of a person's soul potential. By immediately changing the four young men's names, King Neb was, in essence, stealing their identity. Their new names were Belteshazzar (Daniel), Shadrach (Hananiah), Meshach (Mishael), and Abednego (Azariah).

Dietary laws are clearly lined out in Leviticus and Deuteronomy in the Torah (the first five books of the Old Testament). Dietary laws were a call to holiness, and violation was considered a sin. By changing their diet, King Neb was attempting to come between the young men and their God. This was a big sticking point for Daniel. He challenged the chief of staff with a clinical trial:

> "Please test us for ten days on a diet of vegetables and water," Daniel said. "At the end of the ten days, see how we look compared to the other young men who are eating the king's food. Then make your decision in light of what you see."
>
> Daniel 1:12–13 (NLT)

At the end of the ten-day clinical trial, Daniel and his buddies were better nourished and healthier than the other young men who had been captured. (God was with them and blessed their obedience and commitment to Him.) God blessed them with an uncanny ability to learn and retain what they had read and also gave Daniel the ability to interpret dreams. The king was super impressed with their knowledge and abilities and entered them into his service. He found them more helpful than his own employed enchanters and magicians.

One night, King Neb had a disturbing dream and summoned all the wise men of the kingdom to tell him what his dream was about. They replied that they could not possibly know what he had dreamed. He was so angry that he ordered all the wise men to be killed. That night, God revealed to Daniel the contents of the king's dream. Daniel went before the king and told him that all the sorcerers, enchanters, and astrologers could not tell him the contents of his dream, but the God of heaven could. King Neb rewarded Daniel by declaring him the ruler over all of Babylon and the head over all the wise men. (God was with Daniel.)

King Neb must have been a bit bipolar. One minute, he was trying to separate the young Jews from their God, and the next minute, he was worshiping their God. Now, he is back to his old ways:

> Then a herald shouted out, "People of all races and nations and languages, listen to the king's command! When you hear the sound of the horn, flute, zither, lyre, harp, pipes and other musical instruments, bow to the ground to worship King Nebuchadnezzar's gold statue. Anyone who refuses to obey will immediately be thrown into a blazing furnace."

Daniel 3:4–6 (NLT)

When the music sounded, Shadrach, Meshach, and Abednego refused to bow down to the golden idol or worship the god of King Neb. The astrologers were tattle tales and told the king that the three *amigos* refused to bow down:

> Shadrach, Meshach, and Abednego replied, "O Nebuchadnezzar, we do not need to defend ourselves before you. If we are thrown into the blazing furnace, the God whom we serve is able to save us. He will rescue us from your power, Your Majesty. *But even if he doesn't*, we want to make it clear to you, Your Majesty, that we will never serve your gods or worship the gold statue you have set up."
>
> Daniel 3:16–18 (NLT, author's italics)

But even if He doesn't…now that's faith! Shadrach, Meshach, and Abednego had complete faith and trust in their God for deliverance. They had decided beforehand that even if God chose not to deliver them, they were going to remain steadfast in their commitment to Him. *Even if* faith! Do I have that kind of faith? Do you have the kind of faith that *even if* God does not come through the way you have prayed, you are going to serve Him anyway?

Boy, that made Nebuchadnezzar mad! He was so mad that he commanded the guards to heat the furnace up seven times hotter than usual. Hotter than hot. Have you ever seen the furnace that glassblowers use? That is the kind of hot that I imagine the Babylonian furnace to have been. The kind that singes your bangs and eyebrows off when you open the door. It didn't matter, though; he could make it hotter than hot, but their God was still able.

> So they tied them up and threw them into the furnace, fully dressed in their pants, turbans, robes, and other garments. And because the king, in his anger, had demanded such a hot fire in the furnace, the flames killed the soldiers as they threw the three men in. So Shadrach, Meshach, and Abednego, securely tied, fell into the roaring flames.
>
> But suddenly, Nebuchadnezzar jumped up in amazement and exclaimed to his advisers, "Didn't we tie up three men and throw them into the furnace?"
>
> "Yes, Your Majesty, we certainly did," they replied.
>
> "Look!" Nebuchadnezzar shouted. "I see four men, unbound, walking around in the fire unharmed! And the fourth looks like a god!"
>
> Daniel 3:21–25 (NLT)

At once, King Neb ordered the three young men to be let out of the furnace. The young men's hair was not singed, their clothes were not scorched, and they did not even smell like smoke! Why? Because God was with them, and He delivered them in a mighty way.

My life as a single mom wasn't quite that dramatic, but I needed to be constantly reminded that I was not alone. I had my tribe, and I had my God. He never left me. When I couldn't feel His presence, it was not because He left me... it was because I moved.

Satan would love to isolate you. He would love for you to believe the lie that you are in "this" all alone. Your Creator Redeemer wants you to remember that since you are

Imago Dei

imago Dei, you are never alone, and you will never be.

> In those days when you pray, I will listen. If you look for me wholeheartedly, you will find me.
>
> Jeremiah 29:12–13 (NLT)

Chapter 28

The Dance

> For this child I prayed, and the Lord has granted
> me my petition which I asked of Him.
>
> 1 Samuel 1:27 (NIV)

She was five years in the making. We fervently prayed for God's promise to be fulfilled...somehow. I knew in my heart that God would not give my children the desire to be parents if He wasn't going to give them a child. Miscarriages. Failed in vitro attempts. One percent chance of having a baby. But God...

Who would have thought four years ago that my son would be taking his beautiful, spunky baby girl to their first daddy-daughter dance? This past Father's Day, donned in a red poodle skirt, white blouse, lacey socks, and Mary Jane patent leather shoes, and escorted by her daddy, she became the belle of the ball. (Or, more accurately, the sweetheart of the sock hop!) She's three. She's spunky. She's fierce. She knows who Jesus is and loves Him already. Like many promised children in the Bible, when she was born, my kids gave her back to God and promised to raise her knowing and loving him.

The Enemy would like to tell us to give up. He whispers in our ears that God doesn't hear our prayers. He wants us to believe that we've been forgotten. But the voice of truth, King Jesus, tells us a different story. He tells us a true story. After all, one of His names is "Faithful and True" (Revelation 19:11).

> Not a single one of all the good promises the Lord had given to the family of Israel was left unfulfilled; everything he had spoken came true.
>
> Joshua 21:45 (NLT)

> Let us hold tightly without wavering to the hope we affirm, for God can be trusted to keep his promise.
>
> Hebrews 10:23 (NLT)

Satan would have you think differently, but God is who He says He is (faithful and true). God will do what He has promised to do. There are so many examples of promises fulfilled in the Bible that it would take an entire book to recount them all. Author Herbert Locklear actually counted all the promises in the Bible, which numbered 7,147! I don't know how accurate that is, but let's just say this: our God is a promise maker, and our God is a promise keeper!

Nehemiah is one of my favorite books in the Bible. It is a small, obscure little book in the Old Testament that grabbed my heart the first time I read it. I love it because it is a story of servant leadership, which has been my battle cry my entire working career. We start the story with Nehemiah being in a place of leadership, a cupbearer to the king. He enjoyed wealth, power, and influence. He was also a man of God who was deeply devoted, prayerful, and read

God's Word daily. One day, one of his friends from Judah came to visit him. Nehemiah asked him for a report on how things were going in Jerusalem. He learned that things were not going well with the Jews. They were in great trouble, and the walls around Jerusalem had been burned down. In biblical times, if there were no walls around a city, it left the city vulnerable to siege. Nehemiah, being a man of God, understood the importance of protecting God's city and God's chosen people. When he heard the news, he wept, fasted, and prayed for several days:

> Then I said, "O Lord, God of heaven, the great and awesome God who keeps his covenant of unfailing love with those who love him and obey his commands, listen to my prayer! Look down and see me praying night and day for your people Israel. I confess that we have sinned against you. Yes, even my own family and I have sinned! We have sinned terribly by not obeying the commands, decrees, and regulations that you gave us through your servant Moses.
>
> "Please remember what you told your servant Moses: 'If you are unfaithful to me, I will scatter you among the nations. But if you return to me and obey my commands and live by them, then even if you are exiled to the ends of the earth, I will bring you back to the place I have chosen for my name to be honored.'
>
> "The people you rescued by your great power and strong hand are your servants. O Lord, please hear my prayer! Listen to the prayers of those of us who delight in honoring you. Please grant me success today by making the king favorable to me. Put it into his heart to be kind to me."
>
> Nehemiah 1:5–11 (NLT)

What a great prayer! Nehemiah begins his prayer with a declaration of how great his God is. He goes further by praising God for keeping His promises to those who love Him and obey His commands. God is not a vending machine God. We don't put our request in and expect to get the "goods." No, He is a faithful God who keeps His promises when we do our part. He is like any other daddy who loves to give good gifts to His children when they love Him and do what He asks them to do. A command with a promise: love Him and keep His commandments, and He will answer our prayers in His will, in His way...*and* in His time.

Nehemiah prays continuous, nonstop petitions for favor so He can do God's work and restore the city. He prays confessionally. He confesses not only his sins but also the sins of his people and his family. Then, he reminds God of His promise to Moses to return His people to His chosen place if they return to Him and obey Him. Note: eight different prayers of Nehemiah's are recorded in his book. (I would speculate that there are probably several more that he didn't bother writing down.)

Just a side note: there is power in praying God's Word (and His promises) back to Him. I incorporate scripture into my prayers daily. Not because God doesn't remember what He wrote but because I do. It sends the message to Him that I know His Word and that I take Him at His word. Nehemiah did the same. He prayed God's Word and His promises back to Him.

Do you pray for favor? I pray for favor on a regular basis. It's not selfish or narcissistic. It is recognition that He is God, and I am not. It is recognition that apart from Him, I can do nothing (John 15:5). Favor is asking God to do for me that which I cannot do for myself. My obedience is the key to unleashing God's favor in my life. Before every important meeting that I have in my job, I pray for favor. I pray that I will honor God in all that I say and do, and I pray to be innovative and creative and to have listening ears. When a particular meeting goes wonky, I generally can look back and remember that I failed to pray for favor prior to the meeting. I view it as a way to take the meeting out of my hands and place it in His.

Nehemiah understood the importance of praying to have favor with the king. Notice this: he did not move until he had fasted and prayed for several days. In essence, Nehemiah did not jump into battle without a prepared heart and his full (spiritual) armor in place.

One day, when Nehemiah was serving wine to King Artaxerxes, he was asked why he looked sad.

> But I replied, "Long live the king! How can I not be sad? For the city where my ancestors are buried is in ruins, and the gates have been destroyed by fire."
> The king asked, "Well, how can I help you?"
> *With a prayer* to the God of Heaven, I replied, "If it please the king, and if you are pleased with me your servant, send me to Judah to rebuild the city where my ancestors are buried."
>
> Nehemiah 2:3–5 (NLT, author's italics)

Nehemiah is a strategic thinker! He started his request with an acknowledgment of his position and a compliment to the king. *Favor*. Then, he said a quick prayer and asked the king to allow him to rebuild the walls around Jerusalem. His next two requests started with "if it pleases the king." (Nehemiah is a smart guy.) The king agrees to give Nehemiah time off so he can go rebuild the wall. Next, he agrees to send letters ahead of Nehemiah to guarantee him safe passage. Finally, the king agrees to send a letter to request enough timber to rebuild all the gates. I would say that God answered Nehemiah's prayer for favor in a big way!

Nehemiah traveled to Jerusalem and went into stealth mode. He and a few of his men sneaked out at night to inspect the job that needed to be done. When Sanballat and Tobiah (local naysayers) got wind of Nehemiah's plans, they began to heckle him and his men. Application to today: oftentimes, when you step out in faith to do God's work, you will have people who speak negativity into your life. I can remember a time when my husband and I were teaching a small group class for single adults. We knew we were being roasted over lunch most Sundays. But it didn't matter because we knew what God had called us to do. So, if you are coming up against naysayers, do what Nehemiah did…ignore them and keep on keeping on.

> Then I prayed, "Hear us, our God, for we are being mocked. May their scoffing fall back on their own heads, and may they themselves become captives in a foreign land! Do not ignore their guilt. Do not blot out their sins, for they have provoked you to anger here in front of the builders."
>
> Nehemiah 4:4–5 (NLT)

Boom! Not a prayer that I would want to be prayed against me! The work continued. Nehemiah exhibited courage and servant leadership. He reminded his workers that God was on their side and would protect them. He devised a plan of protection while they continued to work. He stayed focused on the task before them and maintained a constant state of prayer. He worked side by side (servant leadership) with his men, with a sword for protection in one hand and a hammer in the other.

> When you hear the blast of the trumpet, rush to wherever it is sounding. Then our God will fight for us!
>
> Nehemiah 4:20 (NLT)

There it is...the promise. "Our God will fight for us!"

> So on October 2 the wall was finished—just fifty-two days after we had begun. When our enemies and the surrounding nations heard about it, they were frightened and humiliated. They realized this work had been done with the help of our God.
>
> Nehemiah 6:15–16 (NLT)

Promise fulfilled. They completed the work. God fought for them. Their opposition realized that Nehemiah's God made the vision come to fruition. God got the glory.

When you are up against it, remember that our God is not only a promise maker, but He is also a promise keeper. The Enemy wants you to believe that God isn't hearing you or that He is indifferent to your prayers. That could not be further from the truth. You are made in His very image, *imago Dei*, and He will fight for you.

Ask. Him. Again.

Chapter 29

Grace Received

> Each time he said, "My grace is all you need.
> My power works best in weakness."
>
> 2 Corinthians 12:9 (NIV)

We have spent the first twenty-eight chapters discussing the lies that Satan likes to tell us about ourselves. It was not an exhaustive list (Satan is quite busy), but I discussed common lies that I have believed about myself, and perhaps you have as well. Satan has been hard at work trying to define us, and we have given the enemy a seat at our collective tables. But no more because we are *imago Dei*. We've talked about the lie, and then we have talked about what God says, the truth. I don't know about you, but I choose to believe the truth.

> Jesus answered, "I am the way, the *truth*, and the life. No one comes to the Father except through me."
>
> John 14:6 (NIV, author's italics)

Three years ago (during the height of the pandemic), my husband and I embarked on a new adventure...we built a house out in the country. Who does that? Who builds a house during the shutdown of a pandemic? Well, we do! (Insert eye roll emoji here.) I would not recommend it, and I would definitely not do it again! We built this house out of a desperate need for fellowship. We wanted a place where people could gather around the table and experience table fellowship. There are several examples of table fellowship in the Bible. Jesus Himself used the breaking of bread to love on and teach others. We designed our home to be a place that is light, open, and with an atmosphere of "welcome." Our plan was to use our home (God's home) to welcome others in, love on them, and serve them. It is our ministry. (Side note: if you would like to read a fabulous book on the importance of table fellowship, check out Amy Hannon's *Gather and Give*.[15])

Shortly after we moved in, we had a few couples over for dinner. Tina, one of my closest BFFs, gave me a wonderfully simple painting for my office nook. It is a primitive painting of a church with the words "Grace Received" printed at the bottom of the painting. It stirred my heart, and it stirred my imagination. *Grace received* really resonated with me. For most of my life, I have struggled with a poor self-image. I have chosen to believe the lies of the enemy rather than the *truth* that my Abba Father says about me. But the good news is that I don't have to believe those lies. In fact, God doesn't want me to believe those lies because I am *imago Dei*, made in the image of God. And you are, too! Our God is gracious and loving and for goodness's sake…He paid a high price for us! Grace rewrites our stories.

> But He said to me, "My grace is sufficient for you, for my power is made perfect in weakness."
>
> 2 Corinthians 12:9 (NIV)

For the next few chapters, we will visit this gift of *grace received* and tie up our time together with a pretty little red bow. (Red because Jesus's love for us was written in red, the color of grace.)

Chapter 30

Grace Begins at the Cross

> And all are justified freely by His grace through the redemption that came through Christ Jesus.
>
> Romans 3:24 (NIV)

The cross is the logical starting place on our grace journey. Back to Sunday School 101. I bet one of the first memory verses that you learned was:

> For God so loved the world that He gave His one and only Son, that whoever believes in Him shall not perish but have eternal life.
>
> John 3:16 (NIV)

Since the mess up in the Garden, sin has separated us from a holy God. Prior to Jesus, for people to be reconciled (fancy word for "right with" God), a sacrifice had to be made to cover their sins. There were so many rules in the Old Testament about the perfect sacrifice, what it could be, and what it shouldn't be. There were rules about when the sacrifice had to be made, where it had to be made, and by whom it had to be made. Gracious! (See what I did there?) There were *a lot* of details! What if you didn't get it right?

I am such an overthinker that I would have been paranoid about the details. (I am also thrifty, so I may have tried to do the pigeon thing instead of the perfect, spotless lamb. Yikes!)

God knew it was too much. He knew there needed to be a better way. Enter King Jesus. Now that I am a parent and a grandparent, I cannot even fathom willingly giving up one of my children or grandchildren to death...for any reason. How does one even contemplate doing that? Father God did it. He loved the world *so much* that He did not want anyone to die and live a life separated from Him. The only way to do that was to send a *once and for all* perfect sacrifice. He sent King Jesus to die for our sins.

> *But God* demonstrates His own love for us in this: While we were still sinners, Christ died for us.
>
> Romans 5:8 (NIV, author's italics)

But God! He didn't have to do it...but He did. Grace runs hard after us. He gave us His *all*. He gave us His *only*. He gave us His *best*. We don't deserve heaven...but grace stepped in, and I am so glad it (He) did. Our first definition of grace is King Jesus. (You won't find that definition in Merriam-Webster's.)

Every morning, I start my day with what we Jesus girls like to call "quiet time." I begin with a series of verses that I recite in my head before I even get out of bed. Ladies, if you want to win the battle for your mind (there is a battle), your best weapon is the Word of God. Hide it in your heart. It is quite handy when Satan tries to shoot his lies of "unworthy" at you. Here is the mantra of verses that I begin my day with. (For the most part, when I memorize scripture, I memorize it in the New International Version of the Bible. For whatever reason, it seems easier to me.) I recite these verses every day. And in this order:

> This is the day the Lord has made. I will rejoice and be glad in it.
>
> Psalm 118:24 (KJV)

> Let the morning bring me word of your unfailing love, for I put my trust in you. Show me the way I should go, for to you I entrust my life.
>
> Psalm 143:8 (NIV)

> Show me your ways, Lord, teach me Your paths. Guide me in your truth and teach me, for you are God my Savior, and my hope is in you all day long.
>
> Psalm 25:4–5 (NIV)

> I am the vine; you are the branches. If you remain in me and I in you, you will bear much fruit; apart from me, you can do nothing.
>
> John 15:5 (NIV)

> Create in me a pure heart, O God, and renew a steadfast spirit within me.
>
> Psalm 51:10 (NIV)

Imago Dei

> In the morning, Lord, you hear my voice; in the morning I lay my requests before you and wait expectantly.
>
> Psalm 5:3 (NIV)

> Blessed is she that has believed the Lord will fulfill His promises to her.
>
> Luke 1:45 (NIV)

> God is within her, she will not fall.
>
> Psalm 46:5a (NIV)

I've got to say that when I don't start my morning with those verses, my mind is usually not right for the rest of the day. Saying those verses is akin to putting on that helmet of salvation that Paul talks about in Ephesians. It is part of my uniform for the day, and it lets Satan know that he has a tough battle for my mind ahead of him. I truly believe that if I had put on that helmet of salvation all those years ago, I would have known (and believed) that I was *imago Dei*. If you truly believe that you were made in the image of God and fight Satan's lies with the truth of the Bible…Satan can't touch that.

> But in that coming day no weapon turned against you will succeed. You will silence every voice raised up to accuse you. These benefits are enjoyed by the servants of the Lord; their vindication will come from me. I, the Lord, have spoken!
>
> Isaiah 54:17 (NLT)

After I say my mantra of verses, I begin my quiet time thanking God for the gift of His Son. I thank Him for running hard after me when I "wandered afar off" (prodigal son reference). I thank Him for bringing me back to Him and to His perfect plan for my life. There is no telling how many blessings I have forfeited over the years, but His grace continues to be sufficient for me.

That reminds me of a story. I don't know where I heard it or saw it, probably from the most reliable source ever... Facebook. (Slight sarcasm.) It went something like this: a saint went on to his final reward in heaven. Saint Peter met him at the pearly gates and introduced himself, "Hi! I'm Peter. Welcome to heaven. I will be your tour guide today." Peter commenced the orientation session and tour of God's mansion. ["My Father's house has many rooms..." (John 14:2a, NIV).] He demonstrated all the features of the saint's room, but he missed what was behind one closet door. The saint asked Peter, "You have shown me all the wonderful amenities of my room, but you have not shown me what is behind that door. I am curious: what is behind that door?"

"Oh!" Peter exclaimed. "That is a closet full of the missed blessings that you forfeited when you tried to do things your way instead of waiting for God's plan to unfold!"

Ouch! I wonder how many blessings I have missed because I got in God's way. Our God is so very gracious and quite the gentleman. He will never go where He is not invited, and He will never force us to choose.

The first choice (and the most important choice) we are given is what are we going to do with His Son, Jesus? Jesus willingly laid down His life for us. He stepped out of heaven and came down to earth as a baby, born in a borrowed barn. He grew up just like any other boy born to a Jewish family, but He never sinned. As an adult, He loved, He healed, He served, He washed feet, and ultimately gave His life for us. The first choice God gives us is to choose eternal life provided through the death, burial, and resurrection of His Son. What will you do with that choice?

God, the gentleman, created us with the ability to choose. With that freedom of choice comes great responsibility. Will I choose to live my life for Him, or will I choose to follow my own way? Will I choose to believe the lies of the Enemy, or will I choose to believe the truth of what God's Word says about me? He did a wonderful thing by creating me in His image (*imago Dei*), but ultimately, the responsibility is mine to believe it.

Chapter 31

I Love Free Stuff!

> For it is by grace you have been saved, through faith—and this is not from yourselves, it is the gift of God—not by works, so that no one can boast.
>
> Ephesians 2:8–9 (NIV)

Clinique has a crazy effective marketing plan: they give away free stuff. It's brilliant! I mean, who doesn't love free stuff? I know I do. Clinique online had me at hello! I order online because they have bonus giveaways going on all the time, plus free (there's that word again) shipping. I know if I spend "X" amount of dollars, I will get their gift, which usually contains about six items plus a cute, zippered make-up bag (of which I have a gazillion). You never know when you are going to need a cute little zippered bag for something, right? Anyway, I usually only need one item, but I comb through the catalog and order a second item. Why? *So, I can receive the free gift!*

Thank goodness grace (salvation) is a free gift. We can't work for it. We can't strive for it. We can't earn it. We don't have to order an extra item to get it. It is totally *free!* *There are no strings attached.* Grace is free. Period.

Satan is a stealth bomber. He likes to fly under the radar

and plant seeds of doubt. He's generally not super overt about it. He doesn't shout. Instead, he whispers in our ears, just like he whispered to Eve in the garden, "Did God really say that?" He plants those seeds of doubt, and we water them and grow them into massive pillars of doubt.

Another name that Satan has been tagged with is *Accuser*. He is the most prolific accuser. He would like us to believe that grace is not free. He likes to remind us of our past sins so he can keep his thumb on us. One of his favorite tactics is to isolate us and repeat his lies over and over until we believe him. "You are unworthy. Look at what you did in the past. You are far too messy to come to Jesus. God does not love you, or 'X' would not have happened to you." On and on the Accuser goes…tearing down your identity in Christ.

> The thief comes only to steal and kill and destroy; I have come that they may have life, and have it to the full.
>
> John 10:10 (NIV)

The above verse is a pretty accurate job description for Satan. His only purpose is to tear you down, tear the kingdom of God down, and eventually take another run at God. He tried that once, and it got him thrown out. We know the end of the story, and we know from Revelation 20 where Satan is going to end up. But he's still trying to take us down with him…literally.

You've heard it said before that the battle for your life is fought between your ears. That is so true. And that is where grace comes into the picture. His grace is sufficient for me and for you (2 Corinthians 12:9). He has given us all the tools we need to fight the battle and win with Him.

I love that there are examples all through the Bible of God's redeeming grace. Just when Satan thinks he's grabbed another one of God's children, grace steps in. When grace steps in, forgiveness and restoration follow:

> The word of the Lord came to Jonah son of Amittai: "Go to the great city of Nineveh and preach against it, because its wickedness has come up before me."
>
> *But Jonah ran away* from the Lord and headed for Tarshish. He went down to Joppa, where he found a ship bound for that port. After paying the fare, he went aboard and sailed for Tarshish to flee from the Lord.

Jonah 1:1–3 (NIV, author's italics)

God said…Jonah ran…a recipe for disaster. You know the story. Jonah knew exactly what God wanted him to do. (Pause for thought: I have always said that I wished God would just provide a flashing neon billboard for me, telling me which way to go. Jonah had a biblical times billboard, but he chose the opposite direction. So…maybe I don't want that billboard? Maybe…I don't *want* to know what direction God is pointing me in. Yikes!) Back to the story:

> Then the Lord sent a great wind on the sea, and such a violent storm arose that the ship threatened to break up. All the sailors were afraid and each cried out to his own god. And they threw the cargo into the sea to lighten the ship. But Jonah had gone below deck, where he lay down and fell into a deep sleep.

Jonah 1:4–5 (NIV)

Jonah was down below deck taking a nap, missing all the drama. The sailors got together and began to shoot dice to figure out whose fault it was that they were about to go down. The dice fell on Jonah, so they asked him what was going on. Jonah had told them when boarding the ship that he was running away from God. (That is a weird intro to his shipmates. I believe I would have denied him passage onto my ship.) Anyway, they asked him what they should do. He told them to throw him into the sea, and the sea would become calm. They didn't want to be responsible for his death, so they began to row as fast as they could toward land, to no avail. They decided to chunk Jonah overboard and begged Jonah's God not to hold them accountable for Jonah's impending death.

> Now the Lord provided a huge fish to swallow Jonah, and Jonah was in the belly of the fish three days and three nights.
>
> Jonah 1:17 (NIV)

Then...Jonah begins to pray. Hmmm...I don't think I would have waited until I was in that stinky fish's belly before I began to pray. I believe I would have begun the prayer of repentance before it came to that...maybe? As soon as Jonah was ingested, he began to *praise God*! Imagine that! Jonah was having a praise party with trash, cigarette butts, beer cans, and dead fish floating all around him. Why? *Because Jonah knew* that God's grace was sufficient for him. He *knew* that his God would deliver him. He *knew* that his disobedience had gotten him into this mess, and he was now ready to do what God had appointed him to do.

> "When my life was ebbing away, I remembered you, Lord, and my prayer rose to you to your

holy temple.
Those who cling to worthless idols turn away
from God's love for them.
But I, with shouts of grateful praise, will sacrifice to you.
What I have vowed I will make good. I will say,
'Salvation comes from the Lord.'"

Jonah 2:7–9 (NIV)

The whale, having suffered from indigestion for three days, began to cough...

And the Lord commanded the fish, and it vomited Jonah onto dry land.

Jonah 2:10 (NIV)

Jonah went to Nineveh and warned the 120,000 townspeople that they needed to repent and turn from their wicked ways, or God would rain destruction down on them. The king of Nineveh heard Jonah's words and declared a time of fasting and prayer for the entire city. God heard their prayers, and their city was saved. (That is not the end of Jonah's story. He becomes a whiner in Chapter 4, and God must deal with that. I'll let you read that on your own.)

The bottom line of the story is that Jonah received God's grace, even after his disobedience. God created us for relationship with Him. He is grieved when we disobey Him and interrupt that relationship. God's grace is fast. God's grace is free. All we must do is say I am sorry and ask for His forgiveness, and He is quick to get us out of the whale's belly. That doesn't mean there aren't consequences to our sins because there are. It does mean, however, that our relationship is restored by His grace, and we can walk forward in peace.

Satan the Accuser likes to beat us up with our sins, but our God made us in His image (*imago Dei*), and His grace is *enough*!

Chapter 32

*The Greatest Invitation **Ever!***

> On the last and greatest day of the festival, Jesus stood and said in a loud voice, "Let anyone who is thirsty come to me and drink. Whoever believes in me, as Scripture has said, rivers of living water will flow from within them."
>
> John 7:37–38 (NIV)

Who doesn't love an invitation? I know I do. I'll admit, it used to hurt my feelings when I would hear about an invitation that had been extended and I was not invited. Yes, I *used to* cry over it on occasion. We all like to be invited; we all want to feel a part. It's not that I really wanted to go; I just wanted to be wanted…to feel included. Truth be told…I am pretty much a homebody. After a long week of work and traveling, comfy clothes and no makeup are just the ticket for me. If you ask me, way too much time and hurt feelings are spent around this whole invitation thing.

These last four or so years, the tabloid headlines and TV news have been consumed with all the Harry and Meghan drama. The big event (the coronation of King Charles) took place last May. The world was buzzing, wondering if Harry and Meghan would be invited to take part in the festivities. Many speculated that the date was purposely set on Prince Archie's birthday so that Harry and Meghan would have a good excuse to miss the coronation. It was funny to hear the British commentators discuss what this means or what that means about the whole invitation business. Personally, I did not lose any sleep over who got invited, who didn't get invited, and who declined the invitation. But I did snag a few hours of the pomp and circumstance of the coronation. After all, I watched every episode of *The Crown* (twice), and I considered myself an expert on the monarchy! LOL!

There is only one invitation that you don't want to miss out on. There is only one invitation that means everything. That invitation is Jesus's invitation to "come." No matter who you are. No matter who your family is. No matter what your background is or what you have done, Jesus extends His invitation for you to come.

God created us for relationship with Him. He created us *imago Dei*, in His image, because He wanted to spend time with us. All throughout the creation story, after each creation, God said, "It is good." But it was only after He created mankind that He said, "It is *very* good." We were intricately woven together and placed on this earth for a purpose. Uniquely crafted by God to abide in Him and with Him. Jesus came to this earth to provide a path to eternal life and to bid us to "come."

Right off the bat, I can think of three instances in which Jesus asks us to come. I want you to notice that in every instance in the Bible where Jesus asks us to come to Him, we are to come to Him just as we are. We are never told that we must clean ourselves up first. We are never told that we must offer some sort of sacrifice first. We are never told that we must come through a mediator. We are told to come *just as we are*.

The first example that comes to mind is what we have

already talked about. Jesus asks us to come to Him so He can help us bear our burdens. Again, I like The Message Version of this verse because it paints a lovely picture of laying our burdens down, abiding in Him, and experiencing His grace:

> Are you tired? Worn out? Burned out on religion? Come to me. Get away with me and you'll recover your life. I'll show you how to take a real rest. Walk with me and work with me—watch how I do it. Learn the unforced rhythms of grace. I won't lay anything heavy or ill-fitting on you. Keep company with me and you'll learn to live freely and lightly."
>
> Matthew 11:28–30 (MSG)

Doesn't His invitation sound lovely? Just as we are. Are you tired and worn out? "Come." I love that. We don't have to get all prettied up or "holied" up. He wants us to come just as we are.

He didn't just say, "Come to Me." He wants us to *get away* with Him. That's interesting. Intimacy grows between people when you get away with them. It's called vacation. A vacation is a respite from all the pressures, busyness, and distractions of everyday life. When I vacation with my husband, we grow in intimacy. (Side note: another way of writing the word *intimacy* is *into me, you see*!) Getting away with somebody is intentional, and it grows your relationship. Jesus wants us to get away with Him so that we can grow in our relationship with Him. Jesus demonstrated rest for us with several examples in the gospels where He intentionally got away with His Father to pray, dwell, and just "be." If Jesus needed that time away with God, then obviously, we do, as well.

Jesus was a carpenter. His earthly father was a carpenter. He understood the importance of apprenticeship. He learned by watching and spending time with Joseph. We call it "on-the-job training." In this invitation to come, Jesus invites us to walk alongside Him, work with Him, and watch how He does it.

When I read the lines "unforced rhythms of grace," the picture of a graceful ballerina comes to mind. They learn to be graceful from practice; it's not automatic. When they do a series of spins, they don't lose their balance and spin-off course because they keep their eyes on a focal point. If I keep my eyes on *the* focal point, King Jesus, I will learn not only about His grace but also how to extend grace.

In this passage, we are also told that He won't ask us to do anything that we were not created to do. We were all created and equipped for a unique purpose. His will is that we walk in what He has created us to do, a purpose that is uniquely our own. To me, this passage tells me that when I walk in step with Him, He will not ask me to do anything that is not within my gifting. There is comfort in that. It would make no sense for me to be on stage at a concert singing my heart out. That is not what I was gifted to do. I am a writer, and I was created to share my heart. Besides… nobody would buy a ticket to my concert (except maybe my mother). LOL!

In the last verse of this passage, Jesus again asks us to spend time with Him. Once again, anytime Jesus repeats Himself in the scripture, we should pay attention to it. We repeat ourselves for emphasis. We repeat ourselves because we mean it. We repeat ourselves because it is an important message we want to convey to our listeners. Five times, He repeats the same message: "Come to Me." "Get away with Me." "Walk with Me." "Work with Me." "Keep company with Me." Can it be any clearer? Jesus. Creator Redeemer.

Good Shepherd. Savior of the world. King Jesus wants to spend time with us!

The second example that I am reminded of is when Jesus tells the disciples to let the children come to Him. In biblical times, parents would bring their children to be blessed. The person extending the blessing would place their hand on the child's head and offer a prayer of blessing. The disciples thought this was a waste of Jesus's time and He had better things to do. Jesus, however, had a heart full of compassion for children and asked for them to come.

> But Jesus called the children to him and said, "Let the little children come to me, and do not hinder them, for the kingdom of God belongs to such as these. Truly I tell you, anyone who will not receive the kingdom of God like a little child will never enter it."
>
> Luke 18:16–17 (NIV)

Two things I get from these verses. First, He *saw* the children and immediately opened His arms and His heart to them. Children who have been outside are stinky and dirty. (Think playground kid smell.) He did not say, "Come to Me when you've had a bath and your nose has been wiped." He wanted the children to come to Him just as they are. He sees us. Just as He wanted the children to come to Him, He wants us also to come. He always extends an invitation. He's a gracious host.

The second thing I learned is that Jesus always finds a teachable moment. This wasn't as much about the children as it was about the adults who were present. He taught them to come to Him with the faith of a child. Children are believers. It's only after experiencing the disappointments that come with aging that they begin to doubt. If we come to

Him with childlike faith, ours will be His kingdom. Come.

The third example of Jesus bidding us to come is found in the last book of the Bible:

> Here I am! I stand at the door and knock. If anyone hears my voice and opens the door, I will come in and eat with that person, and they with me.
>
> Revelation 3:20 (NIV)

Jesus is a gentleman. He will never barge through the door of our lives. He will knock and wait. His desire is to have a relationship with us, but we must let Him in. He will not kick open the door, even though He has the power to do so. He just stands and knocks over and over…because He loves us. I am so glad He continued to knock at my door. I am glad that when I was through doing life my way and opened the door, He walked in.

The second part of this verse is important. Notice there are so many references to dining in the Bible? As we talked about before, in Jewish tradition, when you invite someone to dine with you at your table, you are essentially asking them to be a part of your family. In this verse, not only does Jesus want to enter your life, but He also wants to become a part of your family. That's a big deal!

Jesus invites us to "come." He wants us to get away with Him. He wants us to eat with Him. He wants us to linger awhile with Him. He wants us to come just as we are. What a great invitation…the greatest! We are *imago Dei*…created in His image to have a relationship with Him.

Come!

Conclusion:

The Call

> But when God our Savior revealed his kindness and love, he saved us, not because of the righteous things we had done, but because of his mercy. He washed away our sins, giving us a new birth and new life through the Holy Spirit.
>
> Titus 3:4–5 (NLT)

We have walked along this journey of discovering together that we were created in His image, *imago Dei*. That makes us BFFs because we have been through the hard together. Life is messy. We are messy. But grace, His grace, can bring beauty from ashes. I look back and realize that my life would have been so much different if I had believed what He said about me a long time ago. (I'm still learning—it's a process.) I hope that you grasp just how crazy your Creator Redeemer is about you. I hope that you believe what He says about you and can use some of the verses that we have learned together to combat the lies of the Enemy.

I would be remiss if I did not end our journey together without sharing the good news. If you don't have a personal relationship with Jesus (not just a knowledge of who He is), a new identity can be yours. A new way of seeing yourself can be yours. As I spoke about in the previous couple of chapters, a grace that is greater than all your sins can be yours. All you have to do is ask.

Satan wants you to believe that you are too dirty. Satan wants you to believe that you are unworthy. Jesus, our Creator Redeemer, wants you to know that you are His beloved. He wants you to know that He created you for a relationship with Him…just as you are.

The Bible tells us that we all are messy; we have all sinned. Babies are born sinning. They don't have to be taught how to sin, right? They know right from the very beginning how to manipulate Mommy and Daddy. The Bible tells us in Romans that we are *all* sinners. There are no exceptions (except, of course, Jesus).

> For everyone has sinned; we all fall short of
> God's glorious standard.

Romans 3:23 (NLT)

The Bible also tells us that God, through His only Son, provided a permanent remedy for our sin situation. Jesus got what we deserved to make a way for us to live eternally with Him. (Grace.)

> Yet God, in his grace, freely makes us right in
> his sight. He did this through Christ Jesus when
> he freed us from the penalty of our sins.

Romans 3:24 (NLT)

What's the big deal about living life in sin, especially when you aren't hurting anyone? (One of the Deceiver's favorite lies.) You may be a really good person; the world is full of really good people. Why does it matter? It matters because there is a penalty for sin. That penalty is living a life separated from God. We church people call it spiritual death. Sin separates us from a holy God while we are living here on earth, but after we die, it separates us permanently from God, spiritual death.

> For the wages of sin is death, but the free gift of God is eternal life through Christ Jesus our Lord.
>
> Romans 6:23 (NLT)

Gifts are free. You don't earn gifts. They are yours for the asking and the receiving. God's gift of eternal life is free because of the sacrifice His Son, Jesus, made for you on the cross. He willingly laid down His life for you so that you could live eternally with Him.

There are just three simple things you have to do to receive His free gift, and they will cost you nothing:

> If you openly declare that Jesus is Lord and believe in your heart that God raised him from the dead, you will be saved. For it is by believing in your heart that you are made right with God, and it is by openly declaring your faith that you are saved.
>
> Romans 10:9–10 (NLT)

> But if we confess our sins to him, he is faithful and just to forgive our sins and to cleanse us from all wickedness.
>
> 1 John 1:9 (NLT)

What do you have to do to receive God's free gift? Confess. Believe. Receive.

- *Confess* that you are a sinner and ask for God's forgiveness.

- *Believe* that His Son gave His life as a perfect sacrifice to cover your sin and that He rose from the dead.

- *Receive* eternal life by asking Him for His free gift.

Or…maybe you are like me. Maybe you have been a Christian all your life, but you feel distant from God. Maybe you have let Satan whisper his ugly lies in your head, and you have done life based on his deception. I was the woman at the well. Jesus did not come for a drink of water. He came to give me living water. I was that one lost, lonely lamb that Jesus left the ninety-nine to rescue. I was that prodigal daughter that went her own way, and my Father celebrated at my return. If you are like me…come back. He is waiting for you to stop doing life your way and start doing life His way.

> Are you tired? Worn out? Burned out on religion? Come to me. Get away with me and you'll recover your life. I'll show you how to take a real rest. Walk with me and work with me-watch how I do it. Learn the unforced rhythms of grace. I won't lay anything heavy or ill-fitting on you. Keep company with me and you'll learn to live freely and lightly."
>
> Matthew 11:28–30 (MSG)

Don't listen to the Father of Lies. Don't listen to the world. Forget about what social media tells you. Tune your heart to Jesus. Listen to your Heavenly Father as He calls you to come back. He is head over heels in love with you.

In fact, He rejoices over you with singing:

> The Lord your God is with you, the Mighty Warrior who saves. He will take great delight in you; in his love he will no longer rebuke you, but will rejoice over you with singing.
>
> Zephaniah 3:17 (NIV)

Imago Dei…that's our name.

Soli Deo Gloria

Endnotes

1. Introduction:

Lisa Harper, *Lisa Harper's Back Porch Theology*, Copyright © 2002–2023, AccessMore.com. All rights reserved.

Chapter 5: Call Me Gomer?

2. "Jesus Paid It All." Text by Elvina M. Hall, 1865, Baltimore, MD. Included in All American Church Hymnal. Copyrighted ©1957 by John T. Benson, Jr. John T Benson Publishing Company, Nashville, TN.

Chapter 7: Hey, Big Fella!

3. *Rudy*, directed by David Anspaugh, produced by Robert N. Fried and Cary Woods. Written by Angelo Pizzo. Featuring Sean Astin, Ned Beatty, and Charles S. Dutton. Cinematography by Oliver Wood. Tri-Star Pictures. 1993. 116 minutes. Timestamp of quote 1 hour 30 minutes 21 seconds.

Chapter 9: Ironman

4. David Jeremiah, *The Jeremiah Study Bible.* Copyright © 2013 by David Jeremiah, Inc. Published by Worthy Publishing, a division of Worthy Media, Inc. Worthy is a registered trademark of Worthy Media, Inc.

Chapter 10: 4-H

5. *4-H Pledge*, written by Otis Hall. Adopted first National 4-H Camp. Washington, D.C., 1927.

Chapter 12: Backpacking

6. "I Surrender All." Text by J.W. Van De Venter, 1896. Included in All American Church Hymnal. Copyrighted ©1957 by John T. Benson, Jr. John T Benson Publishing Company, Nashville, TN.

7. David Jeremiah, *The Jeremiah Study Bible.* Copyright © 2013 by David Jeremiah, Inc. Published by Worthy Publishing, a division of Worthy Media, Inc. Worthy is a registered trademark of Worthy Media, Inc.

Chapter 13: The Kid's Table

8. Kristi McLelland, *The Gospel on the Ground.* Published by Lifeway Press® (Nashville, TN) © 2022, Kristi McLelland.

Chapter 14: Walker, Texas Ranger

9. Kristi McLelland, *The Gospel on the Ground.* Published by Lifeway Press® (Nashville, TN) © 2022, Kristi McLelland. Commentary from accompanying video series.

Chapter 15: DQd

10. Merriam-Webster's Collegiate® Dictionary, 10th edition. Copyright © 1995 by Merriam-Webster, Incorporated. Springfield, Massachusetts. Definition on p. 336.

Chapter 17: The Brady Bunch Goes to the Grand Canyon

11. Priscilla Shirer, *The Armor of God,* © 2015 Priscilla

Shirer. Reprinted May 2017, Published by LifeWay Press®, Nashville, TN.

Chapter 20: Masterpiece

12. Alice Walton. Crystal Bridges Museum of American Art, ©2023, Crystal Bridges Museum. Website: crystalbridges.org/about/leadership/alice-walton, quotation from 3rd paragraph

Chapter 22: Lost Luggage

13. Smith, Michael W. "The Heart of Worship," *Worship*, Reunion Records 2001. Track #2.

Chapter 23: Jesus and Naps

14. Ann Voskamp, *Waymaker, Finding the Way to the Life You've Always Dreamed Of*, © 2022 Ann Morton Voskamp (Nashville, TN), W Publishing Group, an imprint of Thomas Nelson.

Chapter 29: Grace Received

15. Amy Hannon, *Gather and Give, Sharing God's Heart Through Everyday Hospitality*, © 2022 Amy Hannon (Nashville, TN), W Publishing Group, an imprint of Thomas Nelson.

Printed in the USA
CPSIA information can be obtained
at www.ICGtesting.com
LVHW011822060224
771120LV00004B/5